The Economics of Target Balances

Hans-Werner Sinn

The Economics of Target Balances

From Lehman to Corona

Hans-Werner Sinn
Department of Economics & CESifo
Ludwig Maximilian University
Munich, Bavaria, Germany

ISBN 978-3-030-50169-3   ISBN 978-3-030-50170-9 (eBook)
https://doi.org/10.1007/978-3-030-50170-9

© The Editor(s) (if applicable) and The Author(s), under exclusive licence to Springer Nature Switzerland AG 2020, corrected publication 2021
This work is subject to copyright. All rights are solely and exclusively licensed by the Publisher, whether the whole or part of the material is concerned, specifically the rights of translation, reprinting, reuse of illustrations, recitation, broadcasting, reproduction on microfilms or in any other physical way, and transmission or information storage and retrieval, electronic adaptation, computer software, or by similar or dissimilar methodology now known or hereafter developed.
The use of general descriptive names, registered names, trademarks, service marks, etc. in this publication does not imply, even in the absence of a specific statement, that such names are exempt from the relevant protective laws and regulations and therefore free for general use.
The publisher, the authors and the editors are safe to assume that the advice and information in this book are believed to be true and accurate at the date of publication. Neither the publisher nor the authors or the editors give a warranty, expressed or implied, with respect to the material contained herein or for any errors or omissions that may have been made. The publisher remains neutral with regard to jurisdictional claims in published maps and institutional affiliations.

This Palgrave Macmillan imprint is published by the registered company Springer Nature Switzerland AG.
The registered company address is: Gewerbestrasse 11, 6330 Cham, Switzerland

Contents

1 **Target: An Obscure Aspect of the Eurosystem**   1
    1.1 The Meaning of Target Balances   1
    1.2 Mirroring the Eurozone Crisis   4

2 **The Target Credit**   9
    2.1 Why Target Balances Measure Credit   9
    2.2 The Decision for Public International Credit   11

3 **Current Account, Capital Movements and Target Balances**   17
    3.1 The Basic Accounting Identity   17
    3.2 Similar Balances in Other Payment Systems   21

4 **The Cash Balance**   25
    4.1 The Measuring and Meaning of Cash Balances   25
    4.2 The IMF's Methodology   27

5 **How the Target Balances Came About: The First Phase of the Crisis**   29
    5.1 The Phases of the Crisis   29
    5.2 Opening the Sluice Gates   33

6 **The Case of Greece**   39
    6.1 The Public Credit for Greece   39
    6.2 Bailing Out Foreign Investors   42
    6.3 Sudden Stop, Capital Flight and Current Account Finance   45

7	**External and Internal Money**	49
	7.1 *Some Definitions and Identities*	49
	7.2 *External Money Crowds Out Internal Money: The Case of Germany*	51
8	**The QE Program and the Target balances**	53
	8.1 *A Liquidity Flood Named QE*	53
	8.2 *The Great Debt Restructuring*	54
	8.3 *The Example of Italy*	57
	8.4 *Triangular Transactions with Investors Outside the Eurozone*	59
9	**The Effective Rate of Interest on Target Balances**	61
	9.1 *Why the Interest Problem Is Relevant*	61
	9.2 *Legal Provisions for Intra-Eurosystem Interest Payments*	62
	9.3 *Pooling: A Comprehensive Way of Calculating Intra-Eurosystem Interest on Target and Cash Balances*	63
	9.4 *Primary Seignorage, Secondary Seignorage and the Definition of the Marginal Effective Rate of Interest on Target and Cash Balances*	67
	9.5 *The Interest Formula*	73
	9.6 *The Currently Negative Rate of Interest on Target and Cash Balances*	77
	9.7 *Compound Interest and the Transfer of Liquidity and Income*	77
10	**Interest Spreads and Tiering**	83
	10.1 *The Interest-induced Shift of Liquidity, Interest Spreads and the Elasticity of Local Money Supply*	83
	10.2 *Differentiating the Interest Rates by Way of Tiering*	85
	10.3 *The Effective Marginal Rate of Interest with Non-uniform Policy Rates*	87
	10.4 *A Lesson to be Learned*	88
11	**The Corona Crisis**	93
	11.1 *The Pandemic Infects the World*	93
	11.2 *The Initial Impact of the Crisis on the Target Balances*	95
	11.3 *The Rescue Measures*	97
12	**The Risks of Target and Cash Balances**	101
	12.1 *Target and Cash Balances were Built Up in Exchange for Goods and Assets*	101
	12.2 *Exit Risks, Exemplified by the Case of Italy*	104
	12.3 *Risks of a Euro Break-Up*	106

	12.4	*Risks without Exits*	107
	12.5	*The Blackmailing Potential of Target and Cash Balances and the Dutch Disease*	112
13	**Conclusions and Policy Recommendations**		115
	13.1	*The Findings of This Book*	115
	13.2	*The Pros and Cons of Target and Cash Balances*	118
	13.3	*Reform Options*	122

Correction to: The Economics of Target Balances — C1

References — 127

Index — 141

Abbreviations

ANFA	Agreement on Net Financial Assets
APP	Asset Purchase Programme
b.o.p.	balance of payment
BIS	Bank for International Settlements
COMECON	Council for Mutual Economic Assistance
CU	Currency Union
CUNCB	Currency Union National Central Bank
ECB	European Central Bank
EDIS	Eurozone Deposit Insurance Scheme
EFSF	European Financial Stability Facility
EFSM	European Financial Stabilisation Mechanism
EIB	European Investment Bank
ELA	Emergency Liquidity Assistance
EPU	European Payments Union
ESA	European System of Accounts
ESM	European Stability Mechanism
EU	European Union
Fed	Federal Reserve System
GDP	Gross Domestic Product
GIPSIC	Greece, Ireland, Portugal, Spain, Italy, Cyprus
i.i.p.	International investment position
IBEC	International Bank for Economic Co-operation
IMF	International Monetary Fund
ISA	Interdistrict Settlement Accounts
LTRO	Longer Term Refinancing Operations
MEP	Member of the European Parliament
MMT	Modern Monetary Theory
NCB	National Central Bank
OMT	Outright Monetary Transactions
PEPP	Pandemic Emergency Purchase Programme
PSPP	Public Sector Purchase Programme
QE	Quantitative Easing
SMP	Securities Markets Programme

SNB	Schweizerische Nationalbank
Target	Trans-European Automated Real-time Gross Settlement Express Transfer System
TFEU	Treaty on the Functioning of the European Union
WTO	World Trade Organization

List of Figures

Fig. 1.1	Target balances 2019	2
Fig. 1.2	The development of Target balances	3
Fig. 1.3	Manufacturing output in selected European countries	6
Fig. 2.1	What is a payment order?	11
Fig. 5.1	Die Target balances and the phases of the euro crisis	30
Fig. 6.1	Public rescue credits for the Greek economy	40
Fig. 6.2	Aggregate public and private consumption in relation to net national income	47
Fig. 7.1	Internal money, external money, and the total stock of base money in Germany	52
Fig. 8.1	Stocks of bonds and refinancing loans of Banca d'Italia as well as foreign securities owned by Italians in relation to the Italian Target debt	58
Fig. 9.1	Policy interest rates and deposits in the Eurosystem	72
Fig. 9.2	The marginal structure of sinks (and sources) of international liquidity flows as measured by the Target and cash balances	74
Fig. 10.1	Interest rates for ten-year government bonds among today's Eurozone countries	89
Fig. 10.2	Percentage of non-performing loans in the total loan-portfolio of commercial banks (2018)	91
Fig. 11.1	Various stock market crashes in comparison	95

List of Boxes

Box 9.1 The rate of return on monetary assets officially assumed for the pooling process   69
Box 9.2 Why the deposit facility rate can be taken to apply to all excess liquidity   70

CHAPTER 1

Target: An Obscure Aspect of the Eurosystem

Target balances result from previous net payment orders fulfilled by the national central banks (NCBs). They constitute claims on, and liabilities with, the Eurosystem and are mostly hidden as "other items" in the respective balance sheets of these NCBs. While the sum of all balances is zero by definition, the positive and negative balances alike have grown throughout the euro crisis reaching values way beyond €1.2 billion, with Germany as the biggest Target creditor and Italy and Spain as the biggest Target debtors. The development of the Target balances mirrors the course of the euro crisis.

1.1 The Meaning of Target Balances

"Target" is the name of an international payment system sustained by the Eurosystem.[1] It derives its meaning from the fact that the Eurosystem is organized in a decentralized manner, consisting of a set of national central banks (NCBs) and the European Central Bank (ECB). The NCBs are owned by the respective nation states and distribute their profits to them, but they carry out the orders of the ECB Council. Target balances measure the sum of net payment orders that have been made between the countries of the Eurozone to buy goods and assets and to repay foreign debt. They are negative for a country that gave these net payment orders and positive for a country whose NCB carried out the orders. The balances are respectively booked as liabilities and assets in the individual NCBs' balance sheets.

The Target balances were very small before the Lehman crisis, showing slightly negative values for countries like Belgium, Greece, Austria and even Germany, while slightly positive values occurred for countries like France, Italy and Spain. But since the outbreak of this crisis, huge imbalances arose with strongly negative values for Greece, Italy, Portugal, Spain, Ireland and

---

[1] Trans-European Automated Real-time Gross Settlement Express Transfer System.

© The Author(s) 2020
H.-W. Sinn, *The Economics of Target Balances*,
https://doi.org/10.1007/978-3-030-50170-9_1

Cyprus (GIPSIC), while Germany, the Netherlands, Luxemburg and Finland showed substantial or even very large positive balances. Figure 1.1 gives an overview of the structure of Target balances by the end of 2019. Note that among the negative balances, the figure includes those of the ECB itself. These balances resulted primarily from net payment orders the ECB made to the NCBs in order to buy assets from their territories. Intra-Eurosystem interest payments on the Target balances that the NCBs pay to one another and that result from the pooling of the NCBs' seignorage income are also recorded in the Target balances. This issue will be discussed in Chap. 9.

The overall development of the Target balances until the end of 2019 is shown in Fig. 1.2. The sum of all positive balances which was equal to the absolute sum of all negative balances went way beyond €1000 billion. By the end of 2019, the sum was €1286 billion, where the Bundesbank alone accounted for €895 billion. The Target balances are the largest single items in some of the NCB balance sheets, often hidden under miscellaneous items, and yet, only a few people understand what they mean.

As this book was completed just a few weeks after the outset of the Corona crisis, a complete set of data showing the effect of that crisis was not yet available when it was due. However, for the Bundesbank, Banco de España and

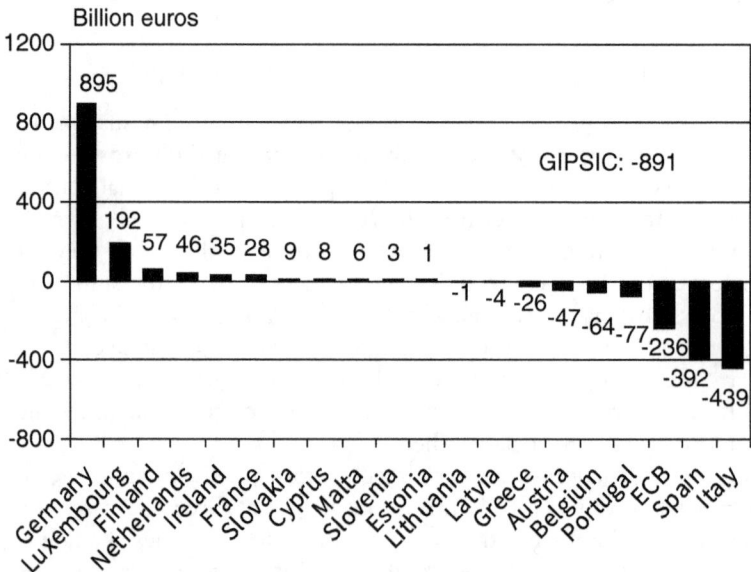

Fig. 1.1 Target balances 2019. (Note: The external countries associated with the Eurozone (Bulgaria, Croatia, Czech Republic, Denmark, Hungary, Poland, Romania and Sweden) are also allowed to have small positive Target balances. They are not included in this diagram. Source: European Central Bank, Statistical Data Warehouse, ECB/Eurosystem policy and exchange rates, Target balances of participating NCBs)

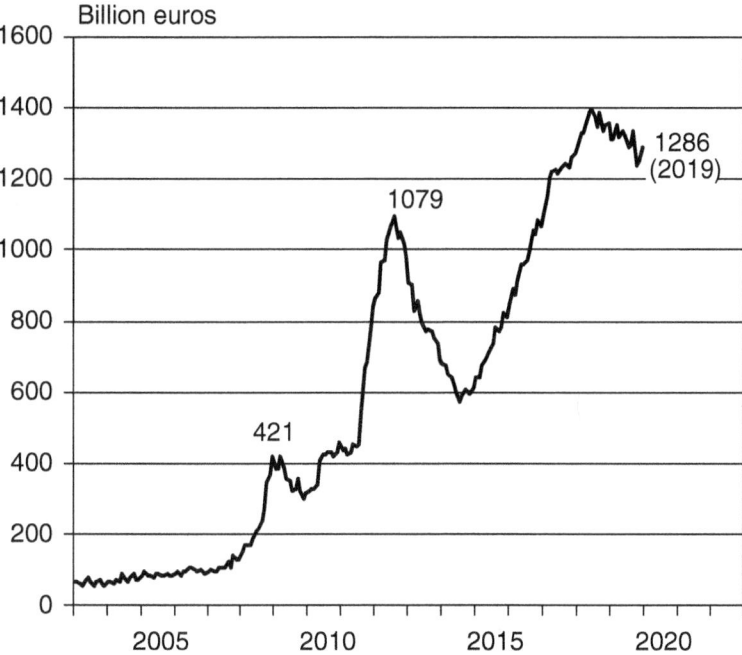

Fig. 1.2 The development of Target balances (absolute sum of negative Target balances). (Note: The graph shows the positive Target balances and the absolute values of their negative counterparts alike, if account is taken of the fact that negative balances may occur not only with individual countries but with the ECB itself while non-euro countries associated with the Eurosystem (Bulgaria, Croatia, Czechia, Denmark, Hungary, Poland, Romania and Sweden) are allowed to participate in the Target system with positive balances. The Target data used in this book refer to end of month. The ECB's negative balances (€236 billion by the end of 2019) result primarily from the ECB's participation in asset purchasing programs. Sources: Sinn/Wollmershäuser (2012), until April 2008 on the basis of a calculation using IMF Data, thereafter: European Central Bank, Statistical Data Warehouse, ECB/Eurosystem policy and exchange rates, Target balances of participating NCBs as well as Deutsche Bundesbank, Banca d'Italia, Banco de España, balance sheets)

Banca d'Italia the Target data covered in this book extend to March 2020 and thus do include the reactions of the respective balances after the first rapid breakdown of the stock market during the Corona crisis. Chapter 5 will argue that the Corona crisis opens up a new phase in the development of the Target balances, and Chap. 11 will discuss what has happened and might still be happening.

Much light has been shed on the Target balances in recent years, but there is an ongoing controversy about their meaning. Are they a normal implication of a well-functioning monetary system or do they indicate financial stress and problems? Do they involve risks for the creditor countries? Are they perhaps even a time bomb for the Eurozone? Or are they the glue that is keeping everything together? Whatever the appropriate answers to these questions, it seems fair to say that they have not yet been well understood by policy makers and even by many experts in academia and in the financial industry.

This is the rationale for this book: It seeks to give a systematic assessment of the Target phenomenon which may counter distorted narratives influenced by vested political interests. The book aims at addressing most of the controversial questions and views that have been expressed about the Target balances. The interpretation as well as the data and facts presented here are partly new, just because the balances have recently been influenced by new policy decisions. However, the book reflects the author's and others' writings on the issue[2] and it also reveals the general scientific knowledge that has accumulated since the rising balances were made known to the public and the economics discipline in 2011. This book tries to be objective, logical and truthful, but at the same time non-trivial, interesting and understandable to non-specialist economists, politicians and people interested in financial matters.

For politicians, Target balances are unpleasant accompaniments of the Eurosystem and make it difficult for them to offer explanations, because the potential policy implications are disturbing, and also because the issue is difficult in itself. The Target balances are therefore often named "meaningless, irrelevant accounting items". However, this view is certainly not correct. It conflicts with the fact that the balances are part of a country's net foreign asset position as published by Eurostat, and their fluctuations enter a country's official balance of payment statistics as public capital export. Former ECB President Draghi said he observes the Target balances "every day actually, not almost every day!" and warned that countries exiting the Eurozone would have to redeem their Target debt in full.[3]

1.2   Mirroring the Eurozone Crisis

Some observers see the balances as a mirror of the crisis if not as a kind of fever thermometer. Indeed, it is noteworthy that the rise of the Target balances coincides with the Eurozone crisis, which broke out in 2007/2008. Whether this mirror interpretation is true or false, it is useful for the reader of this book to be aware of some basic facts about the real economy of the Eurozone and in particular the way it changed when the euro was introduced and when a decade later the world financial crisis broke out in the US and swept over to Europe, igniting in its wake a long lasting Eurozone crisis.

---

[2] The earliest contributions in terms of short policy notes and newspaper articles were Sinn (2011a, b, c, d, e). For more extensive and scholarly early contributions see Sinn and Wollmershäuser (2011, 2012), Sinn (2012a, c, 2013, 2014a, 2015b, d, 2016a, pp. 213–33, 2018a). Homburg (2011, 2012), Schlesinger (2011, 2012), Westermann (2014b). The latest contribution is Sinn (2019b). Further references will be given below.

[3] Draghi (2012, 2017).

The crisis of the Eurozone began in August 2007 when, unnoticed by the general public, the European interbank market broke down for the first time and the first banks came into difficulties, above all French PNB Paribas and German IKK. It culminated with the collapse of the world interbank market after the Lehman crisis in September 2008.

The world financial crisis revealed profound structural imbalances among the countries of the Eurozone. These imbalances became clear, when the world economy and with it the economies of northern Europe recovered in the autumn of 2009 and 2010 while the southern European countries and France lagged behind. These countries suffered from the sudden disclosure of a loss of competitiveness in those sectors of the economy that face fierce international competition. By the end of 2019, twelve years after the outbreak of the financial crisis, the manufacturing output of Italy, Greece and Spain were all still about 20% below the level of Q3 2007. Figure 1.3 depicts the performance of the manufacturing sectors of a selected number of European countries.

Italy, the largest economy in the south, has shown a particularly poor performance. At the time of the Lehman crisis, its manufacturing output dropped by a quarter as did Spain's, and significantly much more than that of Germany or France. Thereafter, until 2010, the country experienced only a mild recovery, much less than Germany for example, and worse, in 2011 a new and serious decline began which caused an upheaval in Italian politics. In the autumn of 2011, Premier Silvio Berlusconi started secret negotiations about a Eurozone exit, but had to resign instead, together with Greek Premier Georgos A. Papandreou, who had had similar intentions.[4] As of 2019, 12 years after the outbreak of the crisis, Italy's overall performance was hardly better than that of Spain, suffering from an output decline of 19% over the entire period. From 2007 to 2019, the stock of manufacturing firms in Italy, net of business start-ups, dropped by 19.4% in net terms.[5]

Arguably, the structural problems that were suddenly revealed when the financial crisis swept over from the US to Europe had been caused by the euro itself, because the euro had created a dangerous economic bubble in southern Europe that ultimately burst. After being announced with a definite time table at the Summit of Madrid in 1995, the euro had wiped out the interest spreads relative to Germany because exchange risks were disappearing and investors believed that, despite the no-bail-out clause of the Maastricht Treaty, bankruptcies would no longer be possible. In Spain, Italy and Portugal, long-term interest rates came down by about 500 basis points, and in Greece they declined even by about 2000 basis points, the rate of interest for ten-year government bonds dropping from 25% to about 5%. This truly dramatic disappearance of interest spreads caused excessive private and public borrowing, which in turn created inflationary Keynesian bubbles that burst at the time of the Lehman crisis. The bursting left in its wake overpriced torsos of once halfway

---

[4] See Bini Smaghi (2013, p. 29) and Djankov (2014, p. 3, 17).
[5] See Istituto Nazionale di Statistica (2020).

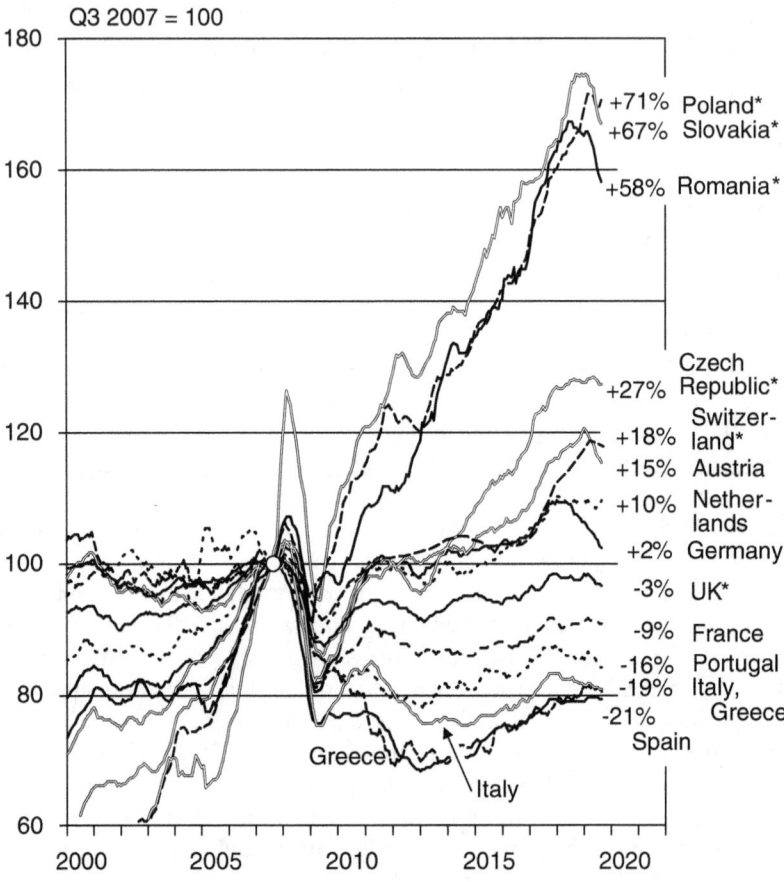

Fig. 1.3 Manufacturing output in selected European countries. *Non-euro countries. (The selection does not include Ireland as the country is the location of huge international distribution networks whose value added data were heavily distorted by rapidly changing profit shifting activities during various phases of the euro crisis that forced a change in the national accounting system. The manufacturing data of Ireland show a rapid, nearly explosive surge of manufacturing output in recent years which can partly be attributed to statistical artefacts due to profit shifting and partly to a genuine improvement of the economy due to a rapid and early real devaluation that fully corrected the pre-Lehman price bubbles. See Sinn (2014a, pp. 122–30) for details. Source: Eurostat, Database, Industry, trade and services, Short-term business statistics, Industry, Production in industry)

competitive economies. As a consequence, the Eurozone has suffered from distorted relative prices of a kind that are usually corrected by exchange rate realignments, which are no longer possible in the Eurozone.[6] Mimicking these realignments in real terms by reverse changes in relative goods prices is possible, but difficult because debtors and tenants with nominally fixed payment obligations cannot adjust and risk becoming bankrupt. All of this was discussed in depth in Sinn (2014a, b, 2015b) and elsewhere, but is not the theme of this book. Nevertheless, it is important that the reader has the basic facts about the real European economies in mind when discussing the Target balances.

This is also true for the Corona crisis, which broke out in China in January 2020 or earlier and transmitted to the rest of the world in February and March, causing an unprecedented post-World-War-II recession. After China recovered, a new epicenter of the crisis developed in Italy, whose hospitals were overwhelmed by the number of sick people arriving. A similar situation developed in Spain. In early April, each of these two countries recorded more deaths than any other country in the world including China and the US. However, as Fig. 1.3 reveals, these two countries were particularly severely hit already by the euro crisis, with a manufacturing output 1/5 below the respective pre-crisis level. The new shock depressing these two countries will add to the financial strain within the Eurozone and result in an unparalleled stress test that the Eurozone will hopefully overcome.

Arguably, there is hardly any variable in the sphere of financial markets that reflects the differences in the tensions national financial markets of the Eurozone face more accurately than the Target balances. That is why it is essential to understand what these balances actually mean in economic terms and why this book was written.

---

[6] See e.g. Sinn (2014a), Chapter 4, and Sinn (2014b).

CHAPTER 2

The Target Credit

Among a variety of potential private and public ways of creating an international payment system for its new currency, the Eurozone chose a public solution without the NCBs, sustaining paid-in accounts. Payment orders from one NCB to another as recorded in the Target balances create open, uncollateralized credit positions that are in fact overdraft credit. There is no limit to this overdraft credit and no settlement mechanism. The latter distinguishes the Target balances from the corresponding (ISA) balances between the branches of the US Federal Reserve System, which are settled annually.

2.1 Why Target Balances Measure Credit

A key for understanding how the Target balances were distorted by the crisis lies in the fact that these balances measure a public international credit provided to, or drawn by, the crisis inflicted economies. When private capital fled and financial strain plagued these economies, they found relief in the automatic stabilization function that the Target credit provided.

The fact that Target balances measure international credit is non-trivial and seems counter-intuitive to many. This is why the analysis of this book begins with this phenomenon. This chapter will not reveal the full story of what happened during the crisis, but try to lay a foundation for the following chapters, which will then explain the details.

Target balances come about by net payment orders between commercial banks that are channeled through, and carried out by, the Eurosystem. The balances are reported as claims and liabilities vis-à-vis the entire Eurosystem. If the ECB itself is included they net out to zero.[1]

---

[1] Apart from the ECB's Target claims vis-à-vis some associated central banks outside the Eurozone such as those of Bulgaria, Croatia, Czech Republic, Denmark, Hungary, Poland, Romania and Sweden.

Payment orders between banks, whether commercial banks or central banks, may, but do not have to, come along with a provision of credit between these banks. And if a payment order is a credit provision, it is an overdraft credit rather than a credit on the basis of a specific contract.

Consider the example of two private banks in the US in the nineteenth century. At that time, the dollar was the common means of payment, but, except for a short intermezzo, there was no central bank. Dollar coins were produced by banks according to well-defined prescriptions about the silver content. Moreover, the common federal state issued bank notes. If the client of a bank D in Detroit wanted to transfer money to the supplier of a commodity in Chicago, C, bank D charged the account of this client and asked the supplier's bank C to pay the supplier the respective sum of dollars. By doing so, bank C (in Chicago) gave bank D (in Detroit) a credit, hoping that there would soon be a countervailing payment order in the other direction. If there was no such countervailing payment order within a predetermined period of time, bank D had to ship gold, silver or federal bank notes to Chicago to redeem the credit it received. This was a risky enterprise as it attracted bandits. The attacks of the bandits later became subject of many Wild West movies.

In 1913 the United States decided to create the Federal Reserve Bank with 12 district banks and an Interdistrict Settlement System (ISA). If there were payment orders between the "District Feds", credit relationships measured by the so-called ISA balances emerged, similar to those between the commercial banks in Detroit and Chicago in the above example. The ISA balances are structurally equivalent to the Target balances in Europe. However, they had to be settled annually by transferring ownership titles in a centrally held stock of gold, which later was placed in the famous Fort Knox. Now the settling of credit claims was safe from the bandits.

The gold settlement system lasted until 1975, when it was replaced with a settlement in terms of ownership titles in a common portfolio of assets that the Federal Reserve System had accumulated by way of open market operations.[2] That system has lasted until this day.

Most other central bank systems are different from these cases insofar as a payment order would not normally imply the provision of credit between banks, as the banks would simply shift existing deposits on accounts with the central bank. The same is true for transfers between two commercial banks located within the same US Fed district. The deposits were given to the banks in exchange for assets or as credit from the local central bank, and they are genuine claims on this central bank that can be transferred between the commercial banks without a credit relationship emerging. An exception is the case where a bank that makes a payment order does not have deposits with the central bank and needs an explicit credit from the other bank that fulfills the

---

[2] A description of the complicated details of the US settlement system including the special role of the Federal Reserve Bank of New York can be found in Cour-Thimann (2013), Wolman (2013) and Sinn (2011d, especially 2012a, pp. 362–69, 2014a, pp. 245–51, and 2015b, pp. 329–37).

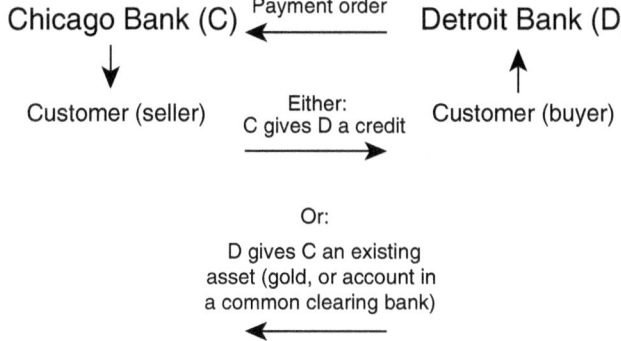

Fig. 2.1 What is a payment order?

order. Normally, however, the former bank would first borrow funds in the interbank market so as to acquire the deposits necessary for the payment order.

In any case, a payment order between banks invariably implies a transfer of an asset between these banks. Either bank C, which fulfills the payment order, gives the ordering bank D a credit and hence receives a credit claim on D, or it receives an existing asset such as gold or a deposit with a common clearing institution like a central bank. Figure 2.1 illustrates the payments and the potential settlement between the banks to help remember the notation.

In international trade theory, the transfer of the asset from D to C—be it an existing asset or a credit title handed over from D to C—is called a capital export in the reverse direction, i.e. from C to D, if this transfer crosses national borders. A net capital export, which by definition is an import of an asset, is normally associated with a delivery of goods and services, unless these goods and services are given away. In the case at hand, the payment order made by D and fulfilled by C serves the purchase of goods from the clients of C. In exchange for the goods being delivered, C receives an asset, and this is called a capital export of C.

The question is now how the payment orders take place in the Eurozone? Do they imply the provision of credit between the NCBs or not?

2.2 The Decision for Public International Credit

In view of the ECB's task of ensuring "the promotion of the smooth operation of payment systems", as defined in the Maastricht Treaty,[3] there were four possibilities of how to construct the Eurosystem:[4]

---

[3] See Article 127, 2, TFEU.
[4] See Sinn (2019a, b).

A. *Private*
International payments are made between private banks or private clearing institutions (with a possibility of mutually lending out bank notes to compensate for physical international currency flows).

B. *European public, with ECB accounts*
NCBs are branches owned by the ECB. All assets purchased with central bank money are properties of the ECB, which itself is jointly owned by the Eurozone's member countries. Commercial banks have accounts with the ECB and are able to make payments among one another by transferring central bank deposits.

C. *National public, with a potential transfer of assets to the ECB to build up ECB accounts*
The assets that an NCB acquires with central bank money are owned by this NCB. However, the NCB can transfer these assets to the ECB to build up a Target account. If it wants to make an international payment order, it transfers the money on its account to another NCB's account. Alternatively, it transfers a corresponding part of its assets to the ECB or other NCBs if it wants to make an international payment order.

D. *National public, without a transfer of assets*
An NCB that makes a payment order to another jurisdiction remains proprietor of the assets it acquired by issuing central bank money. The NCBs mutually provide unsecured credit when they make international payment orders.

Possibility (A) corresponds to the above example of payment orders between the banks in Detroit and Chicago before the foundation of the Federal Reserve Bank System in 1913. According to the Maastricht Treaty, this solution would have been possible. The wording of Article 127, 2 of the Treaty for the European Union (TFEU), namely that the ECB's task is the "promotion of the smooth operation of payment systems" is general enough to also be compatible with a purely private organization of the European payment system. The term "promotion" certainly does not imply that the ECB has to sustain such a payment system itself. Moreover, the plural "payment systems" suggests that the creators of the Maastricht Treaty thought of something very different from the uniform state-run Target system that was ultimately created. This, by the way, is a point of view taken by the former President of the Bundesbank, Helmut Schlesinger, who had participated in the negotiations.[5]

---

[5] Schlesinger (2011, 2012). Schlesinger's contribution was published together with the contributions of other authors, including from the Bundesbank and the ECB, in a special issue of *ifo Schnelldienst* on 31 August 2011, which the author of this book edited to provide a forum to discuss the findings of Sinn (2011b, c, d), Sinn and Wollmershäuser (2011, 2012). An English translation of the *ifo Schnelldienst* volume was published on 13 January 2012 as a special issue of *CESifo Forum*.

Possibility (B) corresponds to the rules applying to payment orders between commercial banks within European countries vis-à-vis the respective NCB. It was not chosen on the European level, as the participating NCBs were keen to preserve their independence and their wealth. They did not want to mutualize their assets under any circumstances and transfer them to the ownership of the EU. From the outset, this was the prerequisite for the introduction of the euro.

To the author's knowledge, possibility (C) was excluded by the ECB Council itself. This may have been the case, because influential political forces wanted possibility (D) or simply because of a lack of awareness of the problems, because significant Target imbalances were not expected, and as Fig. 1.2 showed, this expectation was indeed correct up to the Lehman crisis. This possibility comes close to the Federal Reserve System that was introduced in the US in 1913, except that in the US, a settlement initially took place with gold and today with assets that were acquired by open market operations. It also resembles the treatment of external countries associated with the Eurozone like Norway or Switzerland. The central banks of these countries are able to accumulate Target accounts with the Eurosystem in exchange for marketable assets. These accounts must not be overdrawn.

The ECB Council ultimately agreed on possibility (D). Thus, international payment orders are carried out by the NCBs, and they lead to open positions, because the originating NCBs do not transfer deposits with the Eurosystem or assets they own to the NCBs that carry out the payment orders. In addition, not even the monetary assets that the NCBs received as collateral when issuing new money to the respective economies via the local banking sector are transferred to the Eurosystem. This is an issue that Bundesbank President Jens Weidmann had raised in a letter to President Draghi at the outset of 2012. The Frankfurter Allgemeine Zeitung reported that Weidman explicitly mentioned the growing Target liabilities of debtor NCBs, which had reached a sum of more than 800 billion euros, and suggested a collateralization of these claims. The newspaper also added that his proposal could lead to new confrontations with the ECB.[6]

Indeed, the ECB has no access to the assets that the NCBs have acquired with the base money they issued. The ECB is unable to enforce claims from refinancing credit that the NCBs gave to commercial banks. Further, it does not even have access to the assets that commercial banks gave their respective NCBs as collateral to secure the refinancing credit. NCBs are not merely subordinated branches of the Eurosystem. The NCBs coordinate their policies through the ECB organs, its president, its directorate and its Governing Council, but they are national entities that belong to the respective nation states. As the European Central Bank (2016c) states itself:

---

[6] Ruhkamp (2012a); see also Ruhkamp (2012b).

National central banks are financially independent institutions and fulfill monetary policy tasks related to the Eurosystem's primary role of maintaining price stability as well as national tasks.

Thus, the situation in Europe resembles that of the above example of a payment order that the Detroit bank gave to the Chicago bank in the period prior to the Federal Reserve System. Because, and as long as, the international payment orders do not involve a transfer of other assets between the NCBs, credit relationships between these NCBs arise. The only difference is that in Europe these relationships involve public credit, while they involved private credit in the historical example. Thus, the credit quality of the Target balances cannot reasonably be disputed.

Of course, these are not bilateral credits between the national central banks but between the originating central bank and the Eurosystem, the owners of which—all NCBs together—bear the potential default risk. With a payment order, a bilateral credit relationship initially arises between the central banks involved, but at the end of each day it is converted into a corresponding relationship with the Eurosystem as such.

A single executing NCB, such as the Bundesbank, which has by far the largest Target claims in the euro area, cannot actively influence or even refuse the provision of credit through its decisions. This aspect is important, because otherwise the impression could arise that the Bundesbank was actively involved in building up the balances and behaved incorrectly. This is not the case.

To a limited extent, this also applies to the NCBs that have built up a Target debt. For example, if Banca d'Italia carried out payment orders of Italian debtors to the German Commerzbank because Commerzbank called its outstanding credit claims due, it also had no option to behave differently. If the Italian debtor's commercial banks had sufficient deposits with Banca d'Italia, Banca d'Italia was obligated to replace the private international debt by means of the payment order with its own Target debt and to help exculpate the debtor and rescue Commerzbank whether it wanted to or not. *Indirectly*, however, Banca d'Italia would have been able to react more or less elastically to the liquidity shortage in Italy resulting from the international payment order with new money creation credits, thereby preventing or stimulating compensating private capital flows to Italy. I return to this topic in Chap. 5 and will show that the rules for monetary policy laid down by the ECB's Governing Council do in fact leave an enormous scope for national monetary policy decisions.

The Target credits are undoubtedly loans, albeit of an unusual kind, because although they are redeemable, the creditor NCB, which has a claim against the Eurosystem, cannot call them due, as is normally the case with loans. Only the Eurosystem itself might be able to call its own claims against the debtor NCBs due if the Governing Council makes a corresponding decision. However, the bylaws say nothing about this. The question of the due date is not decisive for the credit status, because consols, that is interest-bearing government bonds without a fixed repayment date, also count as loans. Even normal government bonds do not lose their credit status simply because they are usually never really repaid but are replaced by new bonds when they fall due.

It has been argued that an international payment order from, say Germany to France, would not involve a provision of credit but would simply be the transfer of a deposit that the Bundesbank holds with the ECB to the account that the Banque de France holds with the ECB.[7] The Bundesbank's account with the ECB would shrink, and that of the Banque de France would grow. This view suggests that the Target balances are endowments of deposits on the accounts that the NCBs hold with the ECB. However, this is not the case. Rather, the Target accounts are unlimited and uncovered overdraft accounts whose sum is zero. The accounts are negative if an NCB has made net transfers to other NCBs or to the ECB itself.

This corresponds to the official definition of overdraft facilities according to Eurostat:[8]

> Transferable deposit accounts may have overdraft facilities. If the account is overdrawn, the withdrawal to zero is the withdrawal of a deposit, and the amount of the overdraft is the granting of a loan.

According to this definition, the overdraft constitutes the receipt of a *loan*, a term first used in this connection by Sinn and Wollmershäuser (2011, 2012).

Nothing changes in the correctness of this definition if account is taken of the fact that the NCB carrying out the payment order must make the money transfer to a commercial bank in its jurisdiction, given that this is one of the monetary policy tasks in the Eurosystem. If I have concluded a framework agreement with my bank with an overdraft facility for my account specifying that it has to execute my payment order even if this results in a negative balance for my account, I will use an overdraft loan from it. The obligation to carry out the payment order does not contradict the creation of a credit relationship.

The credit interpretation of the Target balances is difficult to understand by scholars who have not yet familiarized themselves with the nature of payment orders in the Eurosystem. However, in the meantime, leading scholars in the field have adopted this interpretation. For example, the later chief economist of the World Bank, Carmen Reinhart (2017), argued:[9]

> Target2 balances are an external liability of the central bank and in orders of magnitude that are meaningful. Therefore, when we consider public sector debt, rather than general government debt, for Italy, Spain, Portugal, or Greece, those substantial Target2 balances have to be added to that picture.

---

[7] Hellwig (2018b, p. 359).
[8] Eurostat (2010, § 5.82, p. 135).
[9] See also Reinhart (2018).

Aaron Tornell (2018, fn. 1), an economist specialized on currency crises, called Target liabilities "automatic loans from the Eurosystem to a national central bank". Similarly, Tornell and Westermann (2011) named the balances "Eurosystem loans". Aizenman et al. (2019) spoke of "credit lines" that the Bundesbank and other NCBs of "core countries" provided to other NCBs of the Eurozone:

> TARGET2 balances are akin to swap line arrangements implemented via the ECB, where creditor Eurozone countries (mostly Germany and other core countries) provide access to credit lines to the indebted countries (mostly to the Eurozone countries affected the most by the Euro crisis—Italy, Ireland, Greece, Portugal, and Spain).

Finally, even Whelan (2014, p. 101), one of my critics, conceded that the term "Target loans" is a "reasonable" analogy.[10]

After explaining the credit nature of the Target balances, the next chapter turns to their importance for the balance of payments in the Eurozone, because it is the basis for understanding their economic effects and the risks associated with a possible default.

---

[10] On p. 101, Whelan (2014) argues: "A related point on terminology concerns the phrase 'TARGET loans' to describe TARGET2 assets (as used, for example, by Sinn and Wollmershäuser 2012). Because these assets represent a claim on the rest of the Eurosystem that can be settled by payments made at a later date, this terminology can be considered reasonable." Otherwise, Whelan's reasoning has been refuted by Ilzetzki (2014) and Westermann (2014a, b). Westermann accused Whelan of claiming parts of the author's analysis for himself and instead insinuating a number of false statements to him in order to be able to refute them.

CHAPTER 3

Current Account, Capital Movements and Target Balances

The stock of Target balances is recorded in the national accounting systems in the same way as international fiscal credit. A country's Target claim is part of its net foreign asset position, and the increase of this claim is recorded as a public capital export. Intra-Eurosystem interest on Target balances is booked in the country's current account in the same way as ordinary international interest payments. Target balances resemble not only the ISA balances of the US Federal Reserve System but also the special drawing rights of the IMF, Keynes' bancor currency, Soviet transfer rubles, stocks of foreign currency in fixed exchange rate systems and the sovereign wealth portfolio accumulated by the Central Bank of Switzerland.

3.1 THE BASIC ACCOUNTING IDENTITY

The target liability of an NCB measures the stock of net payment orders that this central bank has issued to other NCBs of the Eurosystem and the ECB headquarters. In principle, such orders come about to sustain a current account deficit and a capital export.[1] The payment for the current account deficit includes the purchase of a net flow of goods and services from abroad after deducting the part financed by transfers (gifts) from abroad, as well as net payments for interest, similar capital services and cross border factor incomes. The payment for the capital export in turn serves the acquisition of foreign assets including possible sight deposits with banks, the granting of loans to foreign countries and the repayment of old loans that were previously obtained from abroad. The latter explains the essential part of what is known as capital flight,

---

[1] The term "current account" is used in the literature with two completely different meanings. In the theory of finance it is a demand deposit that a commercial bank holds with its NCB. In economics and in particular international economics it is the surplus of exports over imports, interest payments to foreigners and a few other items in a country's balance of payment. To avoid confusion this book uses the term exclusively in the latter sense.

© The Author(s) 2020
H.-W. Sinn, *The Economics of Target Balances*,
https://doi.org/10.1007/978-3-030-50170-9_3

because repayment is enforced when a loan is due and the creditors do not grant follow-up loans. Capital flight can also prevail, however, if foreigners or domestic residents reshuffle their wealth portfolios from the home country to foreign countries.

International capital flows are mostly private, but they can also result from actions of public entities. When the lenders or capital exporters are public entities, I speak of a fiscal capital flow as opposed to a private capital flow when the lenders or capital exporters are private. In this sense, the terms "private" and "public" refer to the capital exporter, regardless of whether or not the capital importers are private or public. In general, my considerations in this text are algebraic and refer to net amounts. This means, for example, that a current account deficit is a negative current account surplus, a liability is a negative claim, a capital import is a negative capital export and a deficit is a negative surplus. Taking these definitions into account it follows that[2]

$$\begin{aligned}&\text{Target deficit} + \text{fiscal capital import} \\ &= \text{current account deficit} + \text{private capital export}\end{aligned} \quad (3.1)$$

A country's Target deficit is the annual decrease in its Target balance. In a country like Greece, the Target balance is negative and became increasingly negative in the first few years after the Lehman crisis due to a continuing Target deficit. There was a fiscal capital import through the rescue packages, and at the same time the country had a current account deficit and suffered from a flight of capital, thus realizing a private capital export. With Germany it was exactly the opposite. Therefore, Eq. (3.1) applies in reverse, with opposite signs, for countries that are on the creditor side of the Target loans.

Equation (3.1) represents the official posting of the *change* in the Target balance in the European and international balance of payments statistics. The Target balance itself is treated there as part of the foreign assets of an economy and is accordingly included in the calculation of the so-called net foreign asset position, which is the algebraic sum of all foreign assets of a country net of the domestic assets owned by foreigners. It is important to note that interest that an NCB receives from other NCBs or the ECB based on its Target balance is recorded in the current account of the participating countries in a similar way to international capital income flows between the other sectors of the economy.

This is what the ECB says about recording the Target deficit, the Target balance and the interest on Target balances in Eurostat's balance-of-payment (b.o.p) and international-investment-position (i.i.p.) system:[3]

> The changes in the intra-Eurosystem balances (*i.e. changes in Target and cash balances, see next chapter; the author*) should be recorded in the national b.o.p. under 'other investment/currency and deposits/central bank/short-term'; the

---

[2] See Sinn and Wollmershäuser (2011, 2012) or Steiner et al. (2019).
[3] European Central Bank (2016f, no. 3.10.4, p. 59; see. also no. 3.10.3, p. 58).

intra-Eurosystem account should be recorded as an asset when the balance is positive and as a liability when the balance is negative. The TARGET2 account balances should be consistently treated in the i.i.p.

The remuneration of TARGET2 balances should be recorded consistently with the net basis treatment of the TARGET2 balance, that is as income credit when the balance is positive (assets) and as income debit when the balance is negative (liability). The income should be reported under 'current account/primary income/ investment income/other investment/interest/central bank'.

Equation (3.1) shows two important aspects: firstly, the Target loan is at a similar level as that of a fiscal loan granted by the international community to an economy, and secondly, the Target loan and the fiscal loan together serve to finance the current account deficit and private capital exports in the form of investments that residents make abroad including a repayment of foreign loans.[4] The latter was the more important item in most crisis countries in the first phase of the crisis up to 2012. Foreign investors were unwilling to roll over the maturing loans and demanded repayment. In view of the negative current account balances at that time, this could only happen if the public overdraft credit of the Eurosystem, measured by the Target balances, replaced private foreign credits and financed the current account deficits.

Note that the equation describes a definitional relationship from the balance of payments statistics and not causalities.[5] When the capital markets were no longer willing to finance the current account deficits of some euro countries, which had been high even before the Lehman crisis, this funding came about through the Target system. And when there was also genuine capital flight from individual countries, the Target system provided replacement financing. When private capital fled from the crisis countries to Germany and other countries considered safe, the Eurosystem was guiding public capital in the opposite direction. The private capital export of the crisis countries was compensated for and made possible by public capital imports from the Eurosystem.[6]

Without the Target system, there would have been no implicit public capital import from the Eurosystem, which takes place automatically via the Target

---

[4] Sinn and Wollmershäuser (2011, 2012), Homburg (2011), Sinn (2012a, pp. 221–93), Sinn (2014a, pp. 176–251, 2015b, pp. 235–349), Steiner et al. (2019).

[5] My work on the Target balances has occasionally been represented as if I had claimed such causalities, and I was told that even before the Lehman crisis there were current account deficits in the later crisis countries, as if I had said or implied otherwise. Of course, such deficits existed even before the Lehman crisis. My books contain numerous graphs that show this. See Sinn (2012a, chapter 8, 2014a, chapter 7, 2015b, chapter 7). The slopes of the curves shown there are the deficits themselves and do not change at the time of the Lehman crisis. The graphs also show which parts of the deficits were financed by the Target loans during the crisis. An interpretation of causality exists only in the sense that the deficits would inevitably have disappeared when the capital markets were no longer ready to finance them, had the Target loans not been available as a replacement. See Sinn in particular (2014a, p. 212 and p. 219, especially fn. 9, 2015b, pp. 281f. and p. 292 in connection with footnote 11, p. 344).

[6] European Economic Advisory Group (2012, pp. 64ff.).

accounts. If a private payment system had been set up, as described in Chap. 2 (Sect. 2.2, case A), the private flight of capital would have required a compensating private inflow of capital from the banks or private clearing institutions that grant each other credit. Thus, the payment orders to other countries characterizing a capital flight could not, in general, have resulted in a net private capital export. The banks and clearing houses would have charged fees or interest rates high enough for their services to reconcile their willingness to direct capital in the opposite direction of the original capital flight, and on balance there would only be so much private capital export in one direction, as banks and clearing institutions were willing to move private capital in the opposite direction.

Net capital exports would only have been possible to the extent that rising interest rates result in a decline in economic activity which improves the current account via declining imports. This improvement implies a countervailing reduction in external payment orders, making net capital exports possible. However, as capital flight is a stock adjustment and the improvement in the current account only a flow effect, in the short term not much can be expected from this effect, so that the clearing houses and international banks would have to compensate for the capital flight with capital imports.

The private system of payment orders would have been a system of extremely tough national budget constraints. Nevertheless, as a matter of principle, it would have been perfectly compatible with the free movement of capital in Europe, and it would not, as one might think, have implied that one euro in one country would not be equal and immediately exchangeable and transferable to one euro in another country. Tight budget constraints in an economy do not mean that liquidity cannot be shifted freely among economic agents, but that those who are short of liquidity have to offer sufficiently high interest rates or recoverable collaterals of high quality to borrow it. In other words, the tightness normally shows up in interest differentials and collateral requirements and not in capital controls or other exchange restrictions.

However, there is a problem of credit constraints in market economies[7] in the sense that, in extreme situations, rising interest rates beyond some stage might imply that credit will be rationed. This could imply that private clearing houses would not be willing to counter-finance arbitrary quantities of capital flight and impose restrictions on the amount of private capital for which they are willing to carry out the payment orders. The last chapter of this book will study this phenomenon in more detail, and the book will therefore not end with the policy recommendation that the Target system be abandoned. Nevertheless, the reader should be aware that credit constraints are not limited to private payment systems. After all, the public Eurosystem itself imposed such credit constraints in the form of international capital controls in the years 2015 to 2019 in Greece and 2013 to 2015 in Cyprus.

---

[7] See Stiglitz and Weiss (1981).

3.2 Similar Balances in Other Payment Systems

Apart from the US American Interdistrict Settlement System (ISA), which was discussed in Chap. 2, the Target balances show a number of noteworthy similarities with other payment systems that have existed or have been proposed.

One is the fixed exchange rate system with an artificial unit of account and means of payment, the bancor, that Keynes (1943) designed and proposed for the post-war period.[8] Fixed allotments of bancors would be issued by an international clearing system in proportion to a country's external trading volume. Countries that bought more goods and assets than they sold, would lose bancors, which they could replenish by buying bancors from the clearing system against gold. If the deficits persisted, they would be forced to devalue their currencies or impose capital controls. Countries that sold more goods and assets than they bought could be forced to revalue their currencies and/or carry out expansionary fiscal policies. Apart from the gold settlement and the other policy measures aimed at reducing the imbalances, the bancor system showed certain similarities with the European Target system.

In the negotiations about the design of a post-war currency system that took place in 1944 in Bretton Woods, the United Kingdom had officially proposed the bancor system, but it was rejected by the US which instead pushed through a system that would effectively replace the bancor with the dollar and, implicitly, gold. All national currencies had a fixed exchange rate with the dollar, and the dollar in turn had a fixed exchange rate with gold, which was guaranteed by the US Federal Reserve Bank.[9]

Part of the Bretton Woods System was the European Payments Union (EPU), which was created with the support of the US. Within the EPU, Germany had substantial balance of payment surpluses, which led to an accumulation of a large stock of gold.

The payment surpluses first showed up in terms of an accumulation of other European currencies by the Bundesbank, as the system involved automatic and unlimited swap lines between the central banks, forcing the Bundesbank to exchange the foreign currencies for deutschmarks at the pre-determined exchange rate. However, according to a number of international agreements concluded between 1947 and 1948, a growing percentage of these currency claims of the Bundesbank—in the end 75%—had to be converted monthly into gold or dollars, a process that was organized and controlled by the Bank for International Settlements in Basel (BIS). This involved losses for the Bundesbank at the time, as the other European central banks often preferred to deliver gold instead of dollars, given that the market price of gold was below the official parity at which the amount of gold to be delivered was calculated.

---

[8] This proposal is based on a series of earlier papers and letters, starting in 1940 with overlapping and repetitive content written for alternative purposes and sent to a variety of economists and institutions, which are summarized by Moggridge (1980). For an early synthesis see also Schumacher (1943).

[9] See also Eichengreen (2006) and James (2010).

Other payments within the Bretton Woods System also implied that the Bundesbank received gold instead of dollars. Until 1958, when the EPU ended and was replaced with the European Monetary Agreement, the Bundesbank had built up a stock of 2346 tons of gold. The conversion of foreign currencies to gold was thereafter sustained for a while as the market price of gold still remained below parity. When the Bretton Woods System collapsed in 1968, the Bundesbank possessed 4034 tons of gold.[10] In retrospect, a rising gold price had turned the initial losses into profits.

The Bundesbank's stocks of gold and dollars at the time of the Bretton Woods System, especially during the EPU period, was the functional equivalent of its Target claim in the Eurosystem, which totaled €895 billion by the end of 2019. At the current market price, this Target claim was worth 20,591 tons of gold or about 60% of all official gold reserves of the world.

Due to the need to settle the imbalances in Bretton Woods system, the European deficit countries tried to avoid such surpluses from the outset and kept their local money supply tight. This pushed interest rates upwards, limited local borrowing, kept current account deficits under control and stimulated capital imports. The imbalances at the time of the Bretton Wood System were therefore much smaller than under the current Eurosystem, even in relative terms. In 1968, the Bundesbank's dollar reserves were 1.6% of German GDP and the gold reserves were 3.4%.[11] Together these reserves were 5% of GDP. By contrast the Bundesbank's target claims by the end of 2019, €895 billion, were 26% of that year's GDP.

Another example of a Target-like payment system was the one operated by the Council for Mutual Economic Assistance (COMECON) for the Soviet Union, Eastern European countries and other socialist countries such as Cuba and Vietnam. Each state had an account with the International Bank for Economic Co-operation (IBEC), which it could use for payment orders to other states.[12] The unit of account was called the transfer ruble. Because the system did not set limits to the imbalances, the member countries took advantage of it and built up increasing liabilities with the central bank of the Soviet Union and later Russia. In 1992, after the Berlin Wall fell, Russia was no longer willing to deliver unlimited amounts of resources for mere transfer ruble claims. This led to a wave of exits that forced the collapse of the ruble zone in September 1993.

Russian credit to former Soviet republics in the system ultimately accounted for 9.3% of Russian GDP, and debt ranged from 11% (Belarus and Moldova) to 91% (Tajikistan) of GDP. However, the claims and liabilities were not respected when the system collapsed.[13]

---

[10] See Emminger (1986, p. 95f.), and Thiele (2013).
[11] See Sinn (2014a, p. 242).
[12] See Kenen (1991).
[13] See also Wolf and Odling-Smee (1994) and Conway (1995).

Finally, a look at Swiss currency is useful. From 2011 to 2015, Switzerland was in a similar situation as that of Germany at the time in the Bretton Woods system, as long as its central bank (SNB) had fixed the exchange rate to the euro and therefore had to exchange Swiss francs for foreign currency during this period. The overall value of the foreign currency was CHF 218 billion, which was about 33% of Swiss GDP. Before and after that period, it also intervened secretly on the foreign exchange market to prevent an excessive appreciation of the Swiss franc. For the most part, however, it did not keep the foreign currency as demand deposits but used it to buy an international asset portfolio, which among other things made it the largest owner of German government bonds.[14] By the end of 2018, this portfolio (gold + foreign currency investments) had a volume of 806 billion Swiss francs or €713 billion.[15] That was 117% of Swiss GDP, and in per capita terms it amounted to €83,926. Even more wealth has been accumulated by the Norwegian Sovereign Wealth Fund. It amounted to €831 billion in absolute terms at the end of 2018, equivalent to 250% of Norwegian GDP and €156,181 per capita.[16]

The holdings of German government bonds and other investments currently owned by the Swiss central bank are the analogue of the Bundesbank's Target claims in the euro system. The only difference here is that these holdings are marketable and can be exchanged for other assets or consumer goods at any time, while the Target claims cannot be called due and are mere book claims against the Eurosystem and implicitly other NCBs. They can be endogenously reduced if there are reverse flows of goods and assets through market forces, but a single country has no policy parameter by which it would be able to induce the reverse flows.

---

[14] As early as 2012, the Swiss National Bank held around CHF 100 billion in German government securities and therefore financed between 7% and 8% of the German federal debt. See Schöchli (2012).

[15] Gold: 42 billion Swiss francs; foreign currency investments: 764 billion Swiss francs. See Swiss National Bank (2019, p. 164). The data reported in Swiss Francs were converted into euros at the exchange rate prevailing at the end of 2018.

[16] See Norges Bank (2019, pp. 6, 7, 14). The data reported in Norwegian crowns were converted into euros at the exchange rate prevailing at the end of 2018.

CHAPTER 4

The Cash Balance

As international payments may be carried out with physical cash rather than payment orders, physical international cash flows among the countries of the Eurozone may result in "cash balances" that are very similar to the Target balances. Indeed, the Eurosystem makes an attempt to calculate these balances and requires the NCBs to book them in their balance sheets.

4.1   The Measuring and Meaning of Cash Balances

International payments do not have to be made by payment orders between commercial banks and NCBs. They can also be carried out by physically transporting cash across the borders, if this is not prevented by capital controls, as was the case during most of the crisis years for Greece or Cyprus. This creates similar balances and liabilities in the balance sheets of NCBs as well as for payment orders.[1] For example, the Bundesbank had a liability because it had more cash in proportion to the size of the German economy than other central banks. The extra cash issued is recorded in the balance sheet under the name "Net liabilities related to the allocation of euro banknotes within the Eurosystem", in short we can name this a negative "cash balance".

As I will show later, the cash balance is very important for the controversial question of interest on the Target balances, because both balances have the same implications in this regard. The cash balance is defined as the difference between the amount of cash circulating and issued in a country. While the latter is known, the circulating amount of cash ("banknotes in circulation") is only estimated in the Eurosystem by assuming that it constitutes a fixed portion of the total amount of cash issued by all NCBs, this portion being

---

[1] Discussions of the cash liability can be found, for example, in Sinn (2012a, p. 189, 2014a, pp. 92, 270f., 2015b, pp. 221f., 261f., pp. 335ff.), Fuest and Sinn (2018a, b) or Sinn (2018b, p. 30). An early discussion of this issue is offered by Whittaker (2011).

determined by the relative size of the country.[2] Specifically, the relative country size is taken to be the share α_i of the equity of the ECB that was paid in by country i, because this share is defined as the average of the country's population share and its share of GDP, which is only recalculated every five years.[3]

The measurement rule for the cash balance is based on the assumption that a small amount of national cash issued by the local NCB as compared to the size of the economy was caused and enabled by physical inflows of banknotes from other countries for the purpose of buying goods or assets. An NCB that has a positive cash balance can make a claim against the Eurosystem because it is assumed that part of the cash circulating on its territory was created elsewhere by other NCBs lending newly produced money to commercial banks and has flown in for the purpose of buying goods or assets. Accordingly, a national central bank must accept a liability to the Eurosystem if its cash issuance exceeds its size-proportional share of the total amount of cash in the Eurosystem, because it is assumed that the excess cash has flowed to other countries for such purchases of goods and assets.

Germany had a negative cash balance of minus €436 billion in 2019, and the algebraic total of its Target balances (€895 billion) and cash balances was €459 billion euros. Because of foreign workers who bring cash home, the proportion of money that is spent by the Bundesbank and flows abroad has been traditionally quite high. In this respect, the Bundesbank's negative cash balance is not unusual.[4] However, the hypothesis that physical cash actually flowed across the borders in the amount of the calculated cash balance is, of course, a mere fiction, the meaning of which can be discussed.[5] If the over-proportionate amount of cash issued by an NCB is used for domestic circulation only, perhaps

---

[2] However, these are only the banknotes. The nation states issue euro coins on their own account. In 2018, they had a value of 2.30 percent of the total amount of cash (Deutsche Bundesbank 2019, p. 77).

[3] The measurement rule can be found in Article 29.1 of the Protocol on the Statute of the European System of Central Banks and the European Central Bank. The ECB itself is allocated 8 percent of the cash in circulation, which is not inappropriate given the amount of euro cash circulating outside the euro area. It also participates in interest pooling with this share value and, for example, also participates in certain securities purchases as part of the QE program. After distributing a reserve and covering its costs, it distributes its profits to the national central banks. The ECB can generate negative Target and positive cash balances. Associated countries also participate in the Eurosystem, which may only have positive Target balances. These details are complex and will not be discussed here.

[4] At the time of the D-Mark, it was assumed that about a third of the amount of cash issued by the Bundesbank was circulating abroad. See Seitz (1995) and Sinn and Feist (1997). Foreign amounts of deutschmark cash shrank shortly before the currency conversion because the money holders feared exchange losses; they then rose again afterwards. In June 2019, the negative cash balance of the Bundesbank was around a quarter of the base money it had issued (see Fig 7.1 below). The "seignorage wealth", which included the external deutschmark holdings, were socialized when the euro was introduced. It is debatable whether the Bundesbank's current cash liability, which is reflected in the negative cash balance, still results from this socialization.

[5] See e.g. Whittaker (2011), Homburg (2019a) or Sinn (2012a, pp. 189f., 2014a, p. 182, fn. 11, p. 279, 2015b, p. 239 and p. 274, fn. 14).

because this country has different payment habits than others, other central banks would receive an intra-Eurosystem claim and the respective NCB a liability, even though no goods or assets were delivered across borders in exchange. In the absence of other information, this book abstracts from this possibility and assumes in the further analysis that a cash balance will indeed measure an amount of domestically issued cash that has flown to other countries for the purpose of goods and asset purchases.

4.2 The IMF's Methodology

The inflow of cash is technically different from the inflow of liquidity due to international payment orders. Nevertheless, it also is a provision of credit by the local NCB in a similar way as the fulfillment of a payment order does, because the local NCB accepts the circulation of legal tender in its territory that it could have issued itself at no cost. The foreign cash buys the same types of goods and assets that could have been bought by way of making payment orders and results in a similar compensating claim on the rest of the Eurozone, also booked in the NCB's balance sheet. Therefore, it also is treated as a credit-like entity in national accounting systems.

The International Monetary Fund has also recommended a methodology to the European statistical offices that corresponds exactly to the European definition of the cash balance (i.e. the "liabilities related to the allocation of euro banknotes within the Eurosystem"). As the IMF explains:[6]

> From a national perspective, holdings of the CU banknotes issued by a CUNCB in another member economy are external assets [...], even though the currency is classified as a domestic currency.[7]

With these words the IMF proscribes treating the cash balance in international accounting in the same way as the Target balances.

Despite this proscription, however, the statistical systems of the European statistical offices may still be inconsistent on this point, as some side remarks of the IMF suggest. While all NCBs have booked the cash balances in their balance sheets right from the outset, Germany's official statistics only retroactively included the cash balance in the German balance of payments statistics system in 2015, and others may still not have done that. In addition, the reporting of the cash balance in the balance sheets of the NCBs is, unfortunately, not handled uniformly in the Eurozone. While the item is always there in principle, some NCBs lump it together with other balance sheet items, so that external observers may be unable to isolate it.[8]

---

[6] International Monetary Fund (2009, p. 261).
[7] Here, CU stands for "currency union", IIP for "international investment position", and CUNCB for "currency union national central bank".
[8] Some NCBs, such as those in France, Ireland, Portugal and some other, smaller countries, used to show the cash balances in their balance sheets, but have been hiding them since the beginning

According to the national accounts methodology developed by the IMF, the increase in the negative cash balance, specifically the increase in the cash liability due to the disproportionate cash expenditure, is to be recorded on the left side of Eq. (3.1) in a similar way as the Target credit. The modified balance of payments equation, which refers to flows, that is the changes in the balance sheet, is then

$$\text{Target deficit} + \text{cash balance deficit} + \text{fiscal capital import} \qquad (4.1)$$
$$= \text{current account deficit} + \text{private capital export},$$

whereby the term "cash balance deficit" refers to the algebraic annual decrease in the cash balance.

According to the IMF definition, foreign purchases of goods and assets by domestic residents paid with bank notes issued at home are treated in the same way as purchases made with payment orders through the Eurosystem. Both build up a national liability to the Eurosystem and, as explained in Chap. 2, they are public capital imports from the Eurosystem, while the purchase of foreign assets is a private capital export. Any international payment order through the Eurosystem system is a public capital import, and purchases of foreign assets by domestic residents merely swap a private capital export with a public capital import. Both, purchases with cash and purchases by way of payment order make it possible to buy resources (goods and assets) abroad as would have been possible by using private or fiscal loans coming in from abroad. The analogy to the Target balances is therefore mathematically perfect.[9]

---

of 2015, lumping them together with other items which makes it impossible to disentangle them for outsiders. There seems to be much disagreement on this issue behind the scenes. Even the IMF said at the place cited above that it was difficult for technical reasons in Europe to correctly calculate the cash liability. On the other hand, there are countries like Greece or Italy that follow Germany and openly show the cash balances in their NCB balance sheets.

[9] The analogy finds its limit in the event of the exiting of a single euro country if the currency continues to exist. See Chap. 12, subsection "Risks from leaving".

CHAPTER 5

How the Target Balances Came About: The First Phase of the Crisis

Based on the development of the Target balances, various phases of the euro crisis can be distinguished, beginning with steeply rising balances because of a sudden stop and even reversal of capital flows after the bankruptcy of Lehman Brothers, and ending with further jumps in the Target balances due to unprecedented capital flight from Italy during the Corona crisis. The first of these phases was characterized by over-proportional money lending by the Mediterranean NCBs. Over-proportional money lending was necessitated by capital flight and the need to finance current account deficits, and it was enabled by loose local definitions of collateral for refinancing operations, generous provision of local ELA credit and substantial scope left for local money creation under the ANFA agreement. In general, during this phase, liquidity outflows from a country as measured by the rising Target debt was only possible to the extent that over-proportional local money creation and lending by the respective NCB replenished the local liquidity reservoirs.

5.1 The Phases of the Crisis

It has been hypothesized that the high Target claims of the Bundesbank—as mentioned they stood at €895 billion by the end of 2019—can be seen as a natural implication of the fact that the Bundesbank is located at the financial center of the Eurozone. This view may sound plausible at first glance, but it isn't, as it could rather be expected that the NCB located at the financial center of the Eurozone has a preferential access to refinancing credit such that new liquidity is being distributed from there to the entire currency union. Thus, a Target liability of the Bundesbank rather than a Target claim would have to be expected.

Indeed, a situation like this prevailed in the Federal Reserve District of New York that typically held net liabilities in the Interdistrict Settlement

---

The original version of this chapter was revised. The correction to this chapter can be found at https://doi.org/10.1007/978-3-030-50170-9_14

© The Author(s) 2020, corrected publication 2021
H.-W. Sinn, *The Economics of Target Balances*,
https://doi.org/10.1007/978-3-030-50170-9_5

Account (ISA), before the financial crisis changed the direction of financial flows and created positive balances.[1]

The true reasons for the rising Target balances can be understood by examining Fig. 5.1. The figure shows the Target balances of Germany, Luxembourg, the Netherlands, Finland and those of the crisis countries Greece, Ireland, Portugal, Spain, Italy and Cyprus (GIPSIC) since 2003, after the transition to the Eurosystem was completed.[2] Obviously, the curves of the first group of

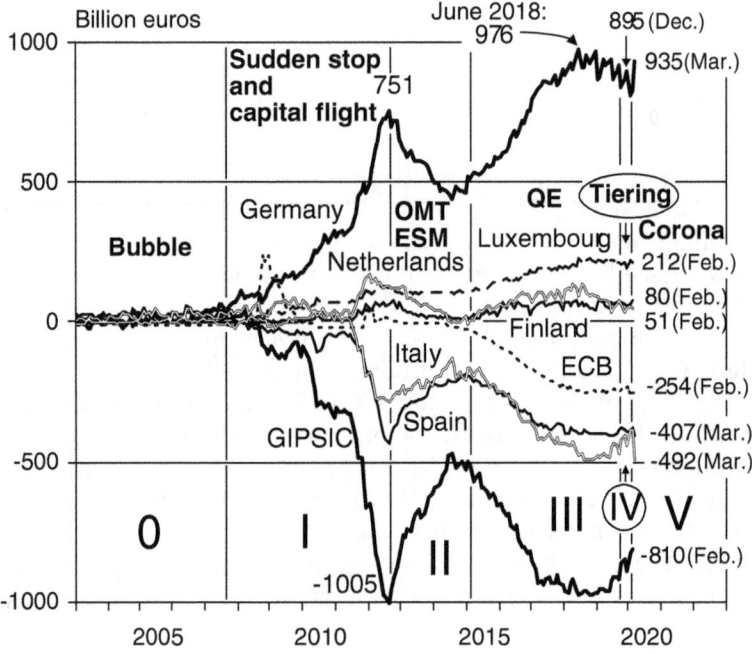

Fig. 5.1 Die Target balances and the phases of the euro crisis. (Sources: Until April 2008, Sinn and Wollmershäuser (2012), on the basis of a recalculation of IMF data Thereafter: European Central Bank, Statistical Data Warehouse, ECB/Eurosystem policy and exchange rates, Target balances of participating NCBs as well as Deutsche Bundesbank, Banca d'Italia, Banco de España, balance sheets. Notes: GIPSIC is the sum of the Target balances for Greece, Italy, Portugal, Spain, Ireland and Cyprus. These are the countries that received public aid through the fiscal rescue packages or through the ECB's Securities Markets Programme. All curves but Germany's end with the year 2019. For Germany it was possible to add two further months before this manuscript was completed.)

---

[1] In the US, the balances are called ISA balances. Concerning the size and sign of the balances of Federal Reserve District of New York before and during the crisis see Cour-Thimann (2013, figure 17, p. 30) or Wolman (2013, figure 2, p. 132).

[2] These were the countries that received aid from the fiscal rescue programs or benefitted from the ECB's Securities Markets Programme, according to which the government bonds of selected Eurozone countries were purchased.

countries are largely mirror images of the second group. The mirror-like development of the other Target balances becomes particularly clear when one looks at the three most important countries that largely explain what was happening: Germany, Spain and Italy.

The graph also shows the Target balances of Luxembourg and the ECB itself. These balances also mirror one another to some extent, both showing a comparatively smooth development. Luxembourg has played a special role as it is the location of the European rescue funds ESM and EFSF as well as of the European Investment Bank (EIB). These institutions issue bonds, large parts of which are bought by the ECB itself. The payment orders from the ECB to Luxembourg create negative Target balances with the ECB and positive balances in Luxembourg to the extent the revenue generated by the bond issues is not fully transferred to the countries to be rescued.

The diagram plays a pivotal role in this book because it demonstrates various historical phases in the development of the Target balances that will be discussed in more depth in subsequent chapters. The diagram distinguishes the pre-crisis phase 0, when the balances did not play a role, and five consecutive crisis phases. As described in Chap. 1, in the pre-crisis phase, a bubble with high inflation rates had built up in southern Europe and Ireland due to the low interest rates the euro had brought. There were only negligible imbalances here because private international capital flows were available across borders to finance growing current account deficits. The imbalances only started with the crisis, and that has nothing to do with the simultaneous change from the first to the second Target system in 2007, which is why this text does not use the term "Target2".[3] Obviously the imbalances rose in cycles with a strongly rising trend.[4] The cycles can be used to distinguish various phases in the evolving crisis and the policy measures taken to contain it. The first phase extended from summer 2007, when the interbank market collapsed for the first time, to summer 2012, when the balances reached a provisional maximum. This phase was characterized by the refusal of the capital markets to finance the long-term current account deficits of the crisis countries any longer, and increasingly also by a genuine capital flight: Foreign investors demanded repayment of loans that became due and refused to provide follow-up financing. Moreover, domestic investors tried to bring their wealth outside the country. Both implied payment orders to other countries, Germany in particular. However, the payments to creditors often initially went to third countries, especially to France, which had become an important credit broker for southern Europe. These third countries then repaid the loans in Germany that they no longer needed.[5]

The second phase runs from summer 2012 to summer 2014. Here, the balances decreased again as capital risked returning to the crisis countries

---

[3] For a discussion of this theme see Sinn (2014a, p. 181f., 2015b, p. 239).
[4] Potrafke and Reischmann (2014) even argue on the basis of an econometric test procedure that the Target balances are "explosive".
[5] See Sinn (2014a, pp. 238–342, 2015b, pp. 323–26, 2016a, pp. 142–47).

because of the ECB's Outright Monetary Transactions (OMT) protection promise and because of the permanent ESM bailout fund.

The third phase began in the early summer of 2014, when the ECB made the first statements about the intended QE policy, which led to a large-scale purchase of securities from March 2015 onwards. In this phase, the balances rose again and already reached a value of almost 1000 billion euros in summer 2018. Chapter 8 will discuss this in more detail.

In the second half of 2019, the Target balances stopped increasing and even reversed their direction. This reversal constitutes a new phase in the crisis that began with the last formal decision under the presidency of Mario Draghi on 12 September 2019. At that date, an extension of the asset purchasing programs and huge exemptions for the penalty interest on demand deposits that commercial banks hold with their respective NCBs were announced. The exemption allowances, the so-called "tiers", were set six times as large as the required minimum reserves.[6] They provided a strong incentive to send excess liquidity back to countries with unexhausted allowances to save penalty interest and hence reduced the Target balances.

The life of the phase dominated by tiering was very short though because in March 2020 the Corona crisis emerged. The horrors of the pandemic forced governments to lock down large parts of the economy and sent shock waves to stock markets, which triggered hectic capital movements across the Atlantic and throughout the Eurozone. Within Europe, again, as in Phase I, much capital was flowing to Germany which was considered relatively safe, implying payment orders that the Bundesbank had to fulfill and resulted in sharply rising Target claims in March. By the end of that month, the Bundesbank's Target claims climbed by €114 billion towards €935 billion in total. The capital came predominantly from Italy, whose economy has been faltering for a long time and which turned into the epicenter of the European Corona crisis. In March, the Italian Target debt increased by €53 billion up to €492 billion. Another Target value known at this writing is that of Spain. The Spanish Target debt increased only slightly in March, by €15 billion and reached a value of €407 billion. In all likelihood other Target balances not yet reported will also have risen in absolute terms in March.

In each of the phases, the shape of the Target curves was also influenced by an interest rate effect on the Target balances, as will be explained in detail in Chap. 9. Up to summer 2012, the balances rose a little further than would have been the case solely due to the effects described above, because interest and even compound interest on the Target balances was booked as an additional Target liability or claim for the debtor and creditor NCBs, respectively. Later, from 2015 onwards, when the policy rates had become zero or negative, this interest rate became negative, and thus there was a mitigating effect on the balances which, if it had operated alone, would have gradually reduced the balances.

---

[6] See European Central Bank (2019c).

5.2 Opening the Sluice Gates

Let us now concentrate on the first phase of the crisis. Capital flight in this phase was enabled and counter-financed by replacing private capital with public capital from the Eurosystem. As explained, this replacement already resulted from the process of making payment orders (and the physical cash transports) itself.

However, while the replacement of private capital by public capital as is implied with the act of making the payment orders as such (recall Chap. 2) or bringing bank notes physically out of the country makes it possible for a country to fulfill its foreign payment obligations, it does involve a local liquidity shortage. After all, each international payment order means that the local NCB withdraws deposits from banks and each international payment with physical bank notes withdraws cash from domestic pockets. As liquidity in terms of base money is necessary for general economic transactions and is thus closely related to GDP, the loss of liquidity resulting from international payment orders and payments with bank notes was normally either retrospectively offset or previously enabled by new local money creation credits issued to local commercial banks by the respective NCBs.[7] Thus, there is a close correlation between the increase in a country's Target and cash balance liability and the local money creation of the respective NCB resulting from the need to prevent liquidity from drying up. Particularly in countries that are already warily observed by capital markets and do not have excess liquidity, this creates a very close relationship between the substitute credit provided by NCBs and the sum of the Target and cash liabilities. It is similar to a lake that has a sluice gate at the top inlet and a drain at the bottom. The increase in Target and cash liabilities directly measures the outflow from this lake, but indirectly it also measures the inflow of new replacement liquidity through the sluice. Only changes in the water level, that is the level of base money circulating in the domestic economy, can temporarily break this connection. However, especially when the water level is low, there is little possibility of intercepting the runoff by further reducing the level. The Target and cash liabilities are then closely correlated with the inflow of new liquidity from the NCB, which comes about through a corresponding money creation credit to commercial banks or a purchase of securities with freshly created money.[8]

The ECB operated the sluices very generously through its policies in order to compensate and enable the outflows caused by capital flight and current account deficits. The Governing Council's decisions created the scope for

---

[7] Sinn and Wollmershäuser (2012), Sinn (2011c, d, e, 2012a, 2014a, 2015b).

[8] The reader may want to check this in anticipation of Fig. 8.1 (introduced below for other reasons) for the case of Italy. The figure shows that the sum of refinancing credit and securities purchases for monetary purposes was very closely correlated with the Italian Target balance until mid-2014, when liquidity was still scarce, but was able to separate itself more and more from the Target path in the following period because the QE program had ushered in a phase of liquidity flood.

national liquidity injections, allowing NCBs to have a say in how much liquidity was offered to local commercial banks, and ultimately these commercial banks decided how much of it they wanted to take.[9] The scope resulted from the framework conditions decided in the Governing Council, such as the full allotment policy and the Longer Term Refinancing Operations (LTROs), but above all from the ongoing reduction in the minimum qualities for the collateral that banks have to deposit with their national central banks, if they want to get refinancing credit.

It is sometimes argued that the NCBs had no leeway to make their own decisions since everything was decided by the ECB's Governing Council. But this is indeed not true for a variety of reasons.

1. The NCBs were allowed to use their own criteria for the collateral they accepted from commercial banks and could even develop their own market segments for securities that were issued and traded in accordance with national regulations. The French STEP market is an example of this. There is a sizable smorgasbord of different definitions for the permissible pledges, which can hardly be overlooked. The conditions were relaxed more and more over time, so that the NCBs were given new scope for acceptable collateral when the better types of collateral on the banks' balance sheets ran out. In addition, thanks to a generous interpretation of the criteria by national banking regulation authorities, ailing banks were able to scratch more and more marginal assets from their balance sheets to serve as collateral. This has all been documented well in the literature.[10] In Greece, Ireland and Portugal, government bonds were still allowed to be pledged, even when the rating agencies had no longer granted these bonds an investment grade. In some countries, banks were allowed to submit as collateral securities resulting from ring trading among various banks which basically meant that there was no collateral. Drechsler et al. (2016) documented that the national regulators had a significant impact on the effects of the ECB's collateral policy. Their summary judgment was that, in Europe, access to the local NCB as a lender of last resort was determined not by the ECB but by the national banking regulation authorities (p. 1970). Thanks to the support of these national authorities, undercapitalized banks were able to borrow more money from the ECB than normal banks, and they managed to place particularly risky types of collateral there, in the purchase of which they had specialized with the help of the ECB. Brendel and Jost (2013) as well as Steinkamp et al. (2017) report that banks in Italy and Spain

---

[9] Sinn (2014a, chapter 5, esp. pp. 147–75, 2015b, pp. 191–234).
[10] See Sinn (2012a, pp. 150–52). Compare also Brendel and Jost (2013), Eberl and Weber (2014), Eberl (2016), Brendel et al. (2015), Sinn (2014a, pp. 153–65, 2015b, pp. 204–14), Weber (2016), who reveal a multitude of other national peculiarities, if not deficiencies, in collateral assessment.

were allowed to submit self-issued bonds because the respective state provided them with a guarantee—a strategy with which Banca Monte dei Paschi di Siena, for example was rescued. Banco de España accepted the papers of "autonomous regions" even if they were on the brink of bankruptcy. Although the ECB claims that the risks would be countered by higher security discounts on collateral, Eberl and Weber (2014), Drechsler et al. (2016) and Steinkamp (2019) showed that the NCBs systematically demanded smaller haircuts for pledges with a poor rating than the market.

2. NCBs were able to declare a state of emergency and issue ELA loans (emergency liquidity assistance) according to their own collateral criteria and without a previous decision or even permission by the Governing Council. This they could only have been denied if two-thirds of the Governing Council's votes objected. In the decisive years of the crisis, however, the six main crisis countries Greece, Ireland, Portugal, Spain, Italy and Cyprus (GIPSIC) had one vote more than a third in the Governing Council and could not be overruled.[11]

3. With their self-made euro money, the NCBs were able to accumulate an extensive portfolio of assets on their own account and to the advantage of their respective states, which collected the profits. In order to prevent excesses, the asset portfolio was limited in 2003 by a special agreement (Agreement on Net Financial Assets, ANFA). But the public only found out about this thanks to the investigative research of Hoffmann (2015, 2016a, b), a doctoral student at the Technical University of Berlin.[12] Sometimes it is argued that the ANFA volume is largely due to historical old assets dating back to pre-euro times. However, this is not true. For one, the stock of historical assets has long been revolved and could therefore have been dismantled had the NCBs wanted to do so.[13] For another, the actual stock of ANFA assets now is much bigger than the stock the NCBs had in their portfolios when they joined the Eurosystem. In fact, the Bundesbank reports that the amount of assets held by the euro NCBs that were not used for monetary policy purposes was around €500 billion at the beginning of the monetary union and had risen to around €1400 billion by the end of 2015.[14] Although the relative importance of ANFA assets has decreased somewhat over time, they still accounted for slightly more than 50% of the Eurosystem's total assets in 2015. Only the

---

[11] Sinn (2012a, 2014a, 2015b).

[12] The European Central Bank (2016a, b, c) published the ANFA agreement shortly after Hoffmann's dissertation had been made public.

[13] The Bundesbank argues that the historical origins of the ANFA items "only play a subordinate role today", because in the aftermath, many NCBs built up their non-monetary assets on the basis of national legal prescriptions and not on the basis of decision of the ECB's Governing Council because they pursued "general investment and earnings purposes". See Deutsche Bundesbank (2016, p. 90).

[14] See Deutsche Bundesbank (2016, figure on p. 90).

smaller part of the assets of the Eurosystem had come into the possession of the NCBs as a result of monetary policy decisions by the joint Governing Council. This is irritating information about the money creation activities of the European NCBs, which for a long time were unknown to the public. The almost tripling of these items during the euro period refutes the view that these are historical legacies that have nothing to do with what is happening in the Eurosystem.[15]

It is true that the increases in ANFA assets appear less dramatic if one deducts the ANFA liabilities, which consist, among other things, of revaluation adjustments and public authorities' deposits with their NCBs that are not counted as part of the money supply. But even if one only looks at the net amounts that embody net money creation, there is still an increase from around €280 billion in 2002 to around €500 billion by 2015. After 2011, the values declined somewhat, but this is apparently to be explained primarily by the Bundesbank's self-restriction, which currently even records a minus position under ANFA, given that it already had to issue enough liquidity by fulfilling foreign payment orders.[16]

The national policy scope implied by the complexities of the collateral policy and by ELA loans, which I described in detail in my euro books, prompted me to critically assess the asymmetrical creation of money in the early years of the financial crisis and to regard it as the result of undercutting the markets by NCBs. After taking note of the ANFA problem, which was unknown to me at the time, my skepticism intensified.

ANFA, ELA and collateral policy enabled the NCBs of the crisis countries to issue disproportionate amounts of euro base money for the provision of refinancing credit to domestic commercial banks or for buying assets from them. This money certainly was not the only additional liquidity with which the net payment orders as measured by the Target balances and the physical cash transports as measured by the cash balances could be realized without local liquidity drying out, but it was part of it.

The assertion that can sometimes be heard that the euro creates debt discipline because a national government must go into debt in a currency that it cannot produce itself—similar to emerging countries borrowing in dollars—is not correct from this point of view. Rather, by stretching the rules of the Eurosystem it became possible for the NCBs to lend disproportionate amounts of self-created money which was recognized as legal tender in other countries and prompted sellers there to deliver goods and assets in exchange.

Specifically, the self-created credit money had various effects in the crisis:[17]

- It served to compensate for and enable private capital flight.

---

[15] See Deutsche Bundesbank (2016, particularly p. 91).
[16] Deutsche Bundesbank (2016, figure on p. 94).
[17] See Sinn and Wollmershäuser (2011, 2012).

- By doing so, it created security for investors and thus reduced the risk of capital flight in the first place (money-in-the-window theory).[18]
- It displaced private foreign credit because, particularly with regard to collateral, it was granted on terms that were not available on the private market. (The ECB spoke of a "disruption of the monetary policy transmission process" that it wanted to compensate.[19])
- It allowed certain national economies to maintain their current account deficits longer than would have been possible given the otherwise forced Keynesian slump and the accompanying reduction in imports, respectively.

In short, the Eurosystem allowed NCBs to asymmetrically create credit money to bail out over-indebted economies whose firms and institutions would otherwise no longer have been able to pay back their debt and to sustain their credit-worthiness, thus limiting capital flight and luring in new private capital. This might be welcomed because it protected the Eurosystem against negative chain reactions that would have caused an even deeper crisis, perhaps with the implication that some countries would have exited and re-introduced national currencies. But one can also take the view that this activity went far beyond the role of the lender of last resort, which Bagehot (1873) meant in his seminal work on the role of central banks, because he only wanted the central banks to fight liquidity crises and not insolvencies and bankruptcies, and therefore insisted that credit to banks must only be given against first-class collateral.

According to Article 125 TFEU, bail-outs are definitely not among the NCBs' tasks. And if they are nevertheless to be carried out, this should have been decided by the parliaments of the euro area. These concerns have not only a firm legal basis but also an economic one, because a bail-out gives investors the expectation that there will be a similar bail-out in the next crisis, which makes them careless and induces them to lend out their funds at excessively low interest rates with insufficient risk premia, which in turn weakens the efforts of the debtors to get their debt under control. The consequence is at least a distortion of the European capital structure with welfare losses of the Harberger type but possibly also a long-term threat to the financial stability of the euro zone, similar to the consequences of the debt mutualization programs under the first American Treasury Secretary, Alexander Hamilton (1755–1804). In the early decades of the US, the mutualization of old sovereign debt reduced the interest spreads and triggered a subsequent avalanche of new debt that led to a bubble that burst from 1835 to 1842, causing a major crisis and bankrupting 9 of the then 29 states and territories.[20]

---

[18] This aspect was stressed by Garber (1998, 1999) when he discussed the transition phase from national currencies to the euro.

[19] The ECB for a long time worked on the assumption that it should not respect country specific risk premia in its policy rates, while markets did. According to standard theory borrower-specific risk premia are necessary for allocative efficiency.

[20] See Ratchford (1941, particularly p. 74f). Cf. also Wright (2008), James (2012a, b, c), European Economic Advisory Group (2013) and Sinn (2014a, pp. 321–23, 2015b, pp. 455–57).

The alternative to opening the money gates to compensate for the flight of capital is to limit this flight by means of capital controls. In fact, Greece imposed such controls in June 2015 and sustained them until September 2019, as this time the ECB closed the sluice. The controls were the last means by which the country was just able to avoid the drying up of its financial system and the collapse of its banks. At the height of the crisis, the market value of a euro "trapped" in Greece due to restrictions on withdrawals from checking accounts was just 80% of the value of a "free" euro in the rest of the euro zone.[21]

---

[21] The former Greek finance minister Yanis Varoufakis conveyed this information to the author.

CHAPTER 6

The Case of Greece

The first beneficiary of the Target credit was Greece. Target and cash balance credit came early in the crisis and was then augmented by the fiscal credit provided officially by the intergovernmental European rescue programs and the IMF. The sum of these credits peaked at €347 billion in 2015 and then declined to €264 billion or 143% of GDP by the end of 2019. Unlike frequent assertions made in 2015, the public credit provided by other states including the Eurosystem and the IMF was not primarily used to bail out foreign creditors. In fact, only about one third of the public credit provided to the Greek economy from 2008 to 2015 was used for that purpose and one third was used to finance the Greek current account deficit accumulated during this period, helping Greece sustain a sum of public and private consumption way above 100% of national income. In net terms, the remaining third was used by Greek investors to finance foreign investment inside and outside the Eurozone.

6.1 The Public Credit for Greece

Despite the capital controls, the Greek economy and its creditors have benefited massively from the Greek NCB's replacement loans, which, as explained, had become possible because of ELA and ANFA credits as well as the Governing Council's collateral policy. At the same time, they benefitted from fiscal bailouts decided by the parliaments, such as the three major bailouts that followed the first crisis.

Figure 6.1 gives an overview of the overall aid provided, updating a graph and using the methodology of Sinn (2014a, 2015b, Chapter 7; 2015a, c, pp. 3–8, 18, 2015d, pp. 3–8, 18).[1] The figure shows the stock of net public credit that has flown to the entire Greek economy. The direct recipients of this credit were the Greek state government and private banks that forwarded this

---

[1] See also Sinn (2012b, 2016a, pp. 236–47, particularly p. 240).

© The Author(s) 2020
H.-W. Sinn, *The Economics of Target Balances*,
https://doi.org/10.1007/978-3-030-50170-9_6

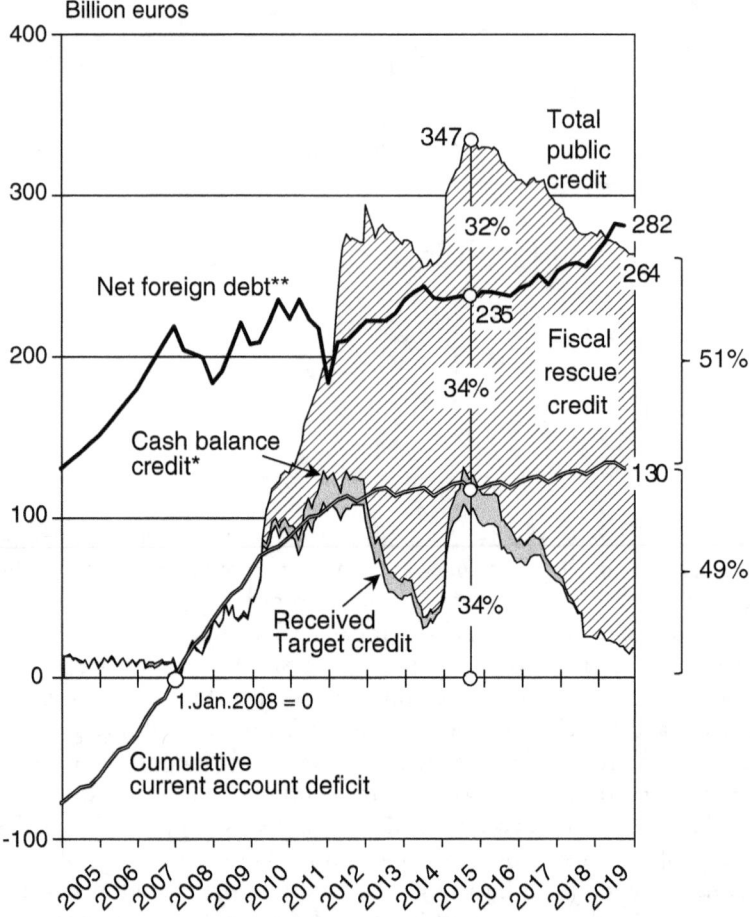

Fig. 6.1 Public rescue credits for the Greek economy. *Liabilities of the Greek central bank to the Eurosystem due to over-proportionate banknote issuance as measured by the deviation from Greece's paid-in capital key. **Absolute value of Greece's negative net foreign investment position. The net foreign investment position is a comprehensive external wealth concept. In addition to all kinds of financial claims and debentures, it includes direct investment, equity stock and real estate, for example. (Note: The fiscal rescue credit is calculated as a net value; it includes the financial help disbursed by the end of each month by the rescue programs of the euro countries and the IMF. The repayments made to date have been subtracted, as well as the Greek contributions to the rescue programs. These include Greece's share in the European Financial Stabilisation Mechanism (EFSM), financed by the EU budget, and also the capital subscription to the European Stability Mechanism (ESM). The most recent data available at this writing were Q3 2019 for net foreign liability and the accumulated current account deficit as well as November 2019 for the cash balance. The other data refer to December 2019. Sources: Sinn (2015c, d, updated), based on data from: Bank of Greece, Financial Statements; European Central Bank, Weekly Financial Statements; same institution, Capital Subscription; European Financial Stability Facility, Lending Operations; International Monetary Fund, Financial Activities; also IMF, SDR Exchange Rate Archives by Month; European Commission, The Economic Adjustment Programme for Greece: Fifth Revue; same institution, EU Budget; European Stability Mechanism, Governance, Shareholders, Eurostat, Database, Economy and Finance, Balance of payments—International Transactions)

credit to the public and private sectors of Greece. Indirectly their foreign creditors will also have benefited. This aspect will be studied in detail below. The suppliers of this credit included the Eurosystem as well as intergovernmental and other international public institutions such as the EU Commission, the IMF and European governments. Keep in mind that the credit is called "public" not because the debtors but because the creditors are public institutions.

The credits are piled up from below. They include the Greek Target credit, the credit in terms of printing an over-proportional amount of banknotes (the absolute value of the negative cash balance) and the various fiscal rescue credits.[2]

The figure shows that the Target credit Greece received was negligible until the end of 2007, but increased rapidly thereafter, if cyclically, when the crisis struck, reaching values above €100 billion in 2011, 2012 and 2015. Behind the net payment orders that constituted this credit was new local money creation credit issued by the NCB of Greece resulting from the loosening of collateral policy, ANFA and, in particular, ELA, which quickly replenished the Greek liquidity losses. In May 2012 the Greek ELA credit reached a value of €126 billion or 64% of GDP.[3] In the Greek crisis of 2015, when Greece again suffered from a massive capital flight and the Greek government negotiated for months about the ultimate payment of another €12 billion from the third public rescue fund, the NCB of Greece again issued huge amounts of ELA credit which eventually peaked at about €90 billion in July 2015.[4]

The local money creation credits of the Greek NCB not only enabled and compensated for liquidity losses due to payment orders, as measured by the negative state of the Greek Target balance (white area, lowest curve). It also materialized in terms of extra bank note printing and subsequent cash outflows, as measured by the dark grey area. As shown above, these outflows, the negative of the Greek cash balance, also qualify as credit from the rest of the Eurosystem, in the methodology of the IMF. This cash balance credit was much smaller than the Target credit but nevertheless significant, peaking at the respective heights of the Greek currency crises of 2011/2012 and 2015. Anecdotally, to avoid being trapped in local bank accounts, Greek citizens with suitcases full of bank notes drove to neighboring Bulgaria to buy real estate. From Bulgaria, the bank notes subsequently may have found their way back to the Eurozone.

---

[2] The graph could also include the net Securities Markets Programme (SMP), which constituted a help for Greece because other NCBs bought more Greek government bonds than the Greek NCB bought those of others. However, as this program qualified as public aid only insofar as it enabled the Greek government to issue more government bonds without offering investors better conditions, it was only an indirect help and was ultimately of negligible importance. It is disregarded here.

[3] Central Bank of Greece, Monthly Balance sheet, item "Other Claims on Euro Are Credit Institutions Denominated in Euro".

[4] Ibid.

Finally, with the height of the light grey area, the graph shows the direct fiscal aid in terms of fiscal rescue credits that Greece received from other states and international institutions. These include a direct intergovernmental aid program of 2 May 2010 as well as loans from the European Financial Stability Mechanism (EFSM), the European Stability Mechanism (ESM), the European Financial Stability Facility (EFSF), and the IMF. All credits are net of redemptions and net of Greece's own participation in rescue programs.

The quantities depicted in the graph show credit stocks at current face values and do not take into account that Greece in addition benefitted twice from an announced interest rate suspension for its government debt with foreign public institutions of ten years each (2012 and 2015). The present value of these two zero interest periods, which are equivalent to outright gifts from the European taxpayers, can be estimated to be roughly equal to about 40 billion euros each.[5]

Up to the end of 2019, the Greek economy received a total credit[6] at face value equal to €264 billion, which was 143% of GDP—and to emphasize again, without the various kinds of debt relief.[7] Just for comparison, the accumulated Marshall Fund aid that, for example, Germany received up to 1952 as a repayable credit was just 5.2% of that year's GDP. France and the UK received somewhat higher percentages of GDP as outright transfers.[8]

6.2 Bailing Out Foreign Investors

It has been argued by former Greek finance minister Yanis Varoufakis (2015) that the recipients of the public international credit were only prima facie Greek institutions. In truth, he maintains, the funds were used to redeem the credit of international investors, banks in particular, which otherwise would not have got their money back from their Greek debtors. The public funds just replaced and rescued the private funds that before had been invested in Greece. Varoufakis put the fraction of the public rescue funds that would indirectly be used to bail out international investors at 90%.

---

[5] For the first debt relief program at the expense of public debtors, the Ifo Institute (2012, 2014) estimated a sum of €39 billion. The characteristics of the second debt relief program decided in 2015 were similar. The haircut at the expense of private creditors in 2012 was €105 billion euros.

[6] For the reasons explained at the outset of this chapter, the overall credit should not be confused with the Greek public debt, which in that same year was 181% of GDP. The public debt the Greek state was able to build up came from domestic and foreign sources which were both private and public. The public credit that the Greek economy received came exclusively from international public institutions and went to the Greek state, the Greek banking sector and the Greek private economy.

[7] The GDP figure refers to 2018, as the 2019 data were not yet published as of this writing.

[8] I am grateful to historian Wolfgang Abelshauser, University of Bielefeld, for this information. Cf. also Abelshauser (2017). Similar figures (5.5% of the 1952 GDP for the accumulated Marshall credits) are reported by Berger and Ritschl (1995, Table on p. 479). It should be noted though that at the London debt agreement of 1952, Germany benefitted from a debt relief worth 22% of that year's GPD. See Buchheim (1986).

The view expressed by Varoufakis certainly has a core of truth insofar as foreign investors were certainly happy about the bail-outs. And it is probably true that they were politically the main driving forces behind the rescue operations, hiding their vested interest by pointing to the misery of poor Greeks. French banks in particular were heavily invested in Greece, and it was France that pushed through the rescue operations in early 2010 against the initial opposition of Germany.

Without the public credit from the printing press and the community of states, even more haircuts than the one of €105 billion at the expense of private Greek investors in early 2012 would have been necessary, and even more severe wealth losses with bank failures would have occurred.

Yet, the quantitative part of Varoufakis' statement may stand on a more unsure ground. Was it really 90% of the funds that went to foreign investors? Figure 6.1 clarifies this question.

In principle, the public credits (Target, cash balance and fiscal) could have been used for three purposes:

- financing the current account deficits,
- financing a repayment of foreign loans and securities that became due (bail out) and
- financing foreign investment by Greek investors.

To find out how important these purposes were empirically, Fig. 6.1 contains two further curves. The first one, the double lined curve, is the accumulated current account deficit of Greece, the accumulation beginning with 1 January of the Lehman year 2008, where the curve by design cuts the abscissa from below. The slope of this curve is the respective current account deficit of Greece. Note that the slope does not change when the curve cuts the abscissa. This makes it clear that the current account did not change when the crisis broke out and the Target imbalances started.

The second, solid curve higher up shows the net foreign liability of the entire Greek economy which I define here as the absolute value of the country's (negative) net foreign investment position. The net foreign investment position of a country is the sum of all possessions and claims that domestic residents and institutions hold abroad or against foreign debtors net of the respective sum of all claims and possessions that foreign residents and institutions hold in this country or against its residents and institutions. Being a broad macroeconomic concept, it not only includes financial claims in the narrower sense, but also wealth titles resulting from direct investment and the acquisition of equity stock, real estate and other non-financial investment.

Both the net foreign liability curve and the curve showing the accumulated current account deficit are related but not identical, as the latter is the sum of all previous current account deficits, not just those since 2008. Moreover, the net foreign liability curve also reflects devaluation and revaluation effects for the assets Greece handed over to foreign investors in exchange of the current account deficits.

Note first that the net foreign liability of Greece towards[9] the end of 2019 was €282 billion while the overall net public credit Greece had received during the crisis was the above-mentioned €264 billion. Thus, indeed, 94% of the entire foreign net liability had become public debt. So, at first glance this seems to support Varoufakis.

However, it should not be overlooked that according to Fig. 6.1, during the crisis up to the end of 2019, €130 billion new foreign liability was created through current account deficits and thus helped to finance the Greek living standard. About half (49%) of the entire public rescue credit Greece received was absorbed by the current account deficits. Only the other half (51%) might have been used to bail out foreign investors, although not even that is clear, as some of these funds may have been used by Greek investors to finance foreign investments rather than for redeeming old liabilities that existed already before the crisis. Thus, the claim that 90% of the rescue credit was used to bail out foreign investors cannot be confirmed.

To be fair, Varoufakis made his statement in 2015 and he must therefore have referred to earlier data. However, the situation at that time does not give more support to his view, because 2015 was the year in which the Greek crisis had culminated a second time after the first peak in 2012. As the percentage figures at the vertical line show, at that time 34% of the entire rescue credit had been used for financing the Greek current account during the crisis, and only 34% was used for a potential bail-out of foreign investors. Interestingly enough, the sum of all public rescue credits was €347 billion which was much bigger than the entire net foreign liability of Greece including the liability from public rescue credits[10] which stood at €235 billion. In net terms, the difference, €112 billion or 32% of the total public rescue credit including the help from the Eurosystem, must have been used to finance foreign investments by Greek investors. Roughly speaking, one third of the rescue funds were thus used to finance the Greek living standard in terms of the current account deficit, one third to finance a bail-out of foreign investors and one third to finance foreign investments by Greek investors during the crisis.

A qualification is appropriate here insofar as all statements refer to net rather than gross figures. It may well be the case, of course, that more than the stated amount of €112 billion was used for foreign investment if at the same time foreigners invested in Greece. And of course the recipients of the rescue funds—banks and the government—will not have used the funds directly for investing them abroad. Thus, for example, banks were able to provide loans to Greek investors who then could use the money for foreign investment, and the government may have used its funds to replace missing tax revenues that

---

[9] See the explanatory note below Fig. 2.1

[10] Recall from Chaps. 3 and 4 that a country's Target and cash balances are included in its net foreign investment position, and of course the fiscal rescue credits were also included.

sustained incomes in the private economy with which foreign investment could be financed. Behind the net figures shown in the graph, there is a myriad of potential financial flows involving a multitude of agents that would be hard to disentangle empirically.

The reader should moreover be aware of the fact that the net foreign liability position is subject to re- and devaluation effects due to changing market prices and haircuts. Thus, for example, the decline in the net foreign liability in the winter 2011/2012 reflects the sharp devaluation of Greece's government debt titles including a €105 billion haircut at the expense of private investors.[11] The resulting increase in the overhang of public credit over the net foreign liability of Greece in this case clearly was not the result of deliberate foreign investment by Greek citizens, but of an involuntary gift by foreigners.

That being said, the situation in 2015 is nevertheless obvious. The net foreign liability curve showed no particular fluctuations at that time, but nevertheless overall public credit was shooting up way beyond net foreign liability. Target debt and cash balance debt increased due to capital flight, which was counter-financed and made possible by a surge of ELA credit. To the extent that the increase in public debt surpassed net foreign liability, it not only was used to redeem existing foreign debt titles held by private investors but to actually invest abroad. This is in line with reports about the enormous external activities of Greek investors during the crisis. There are well-documented reports, for example, of their activities in the London and Berlin real estate markets, where Greek investment funds were even advertising in public media that they were looking for objects to buy.[12]

6.3 Sudden Stop, Capital Flight and Current Account Finance

It is also disturbing to see how important the Eurosystem's overdraft credits in the form of negative Target and cash balances were for financing the Greek current account deficit at times when there was no capital flight. Obviously, in Fig. 6.1 the current account curve coincides more or less with the curve of the Target balance in the first years of the crisis until the beginning of 2010, which itself was flat and close to zero before 2008. In the first two years of the crisis, the accumulated current account was roughly equal to the new Greek Target debt which, as was explained in the previous chapter, indirectly measures the extra liquidity coming from money creation credit provided by the Greek NCB. During this period, there was no capital flight yet in the sense that existing foreign capital was called back home or that Greek investors tried to leave the country, because in such a case the curve showing the aggregate sum of rescue credits from all sources would have had to exceed the curve showing the accumulated current account. Without building up more Target and cash

---
[11] See Sinn (2014a, Figure 2.3, p. 46).
[12] See Focus Online (2011) and faz.net (2012).

balances and receiving additional other public credit from abroad than was absorbed by the current account deficit, there would have been no money to finance a net capital export. Thus one may say that in this period Greece financed its entire current account deficit with the printing press, because the inflow of private credit funds from abroad that had financed this deficit before 2008 suddenly stopped.[13]

Given that the curves shown refer to macroeconomic aggregates, the reader should be warned not to over-interpret this result. It is not meant, for example, to say that banks or governments bought more imported goods, thus causing current account deficits, because they had received more public credit. This cannot be true as the current accounts did not change much in these years relative to the situation before 2008, and both agents are not the typical buyers of imports anyway. Neither does it mean that governments were lending funds to households or firms so that they were buyers. What it does mean is that banks replaced interbank credit they had received in the European market with credit from the Greek NCB and that governments received fiscal rescue funds from abroad that they could use to continue paying for pensions, wages and public procurement, which enabled the recipients to continue buying their normal quantities of import goods.

In addition to financing current account deficits, the public credit was used to compensate for outright capital flight. But that began only in 2010. As Fig. 6.1 shows, from 2010 onwards the curve showing the sum of the Target balance, the cash balance and the fiscal rescue credit, increasingly exceeded the curve of the accumulated current account deficit. The excess of the public credit over the current account curve which began in spring 2010 is the bail-out of foreign creditors to which Varoufakis alluded. The bail-out was a capital flight of foreign investors back home or to other locations outside Greece.

In the autumn of 2011 the capital flight had become so intense that the public credit curve surpassed the curve showing the entire Greek foreign liability position, including this credit. Now, the public credit enabled Greek citizens and institutions to invest in net terms abroad, which meant that they either bought new assets abroad or were protected from selling existing foreign assets to redeem their debt. Still, the financing of the current account deficit and hence sustaining the living standard of the population despite the collapse of the economy (recall Fig. 1.3 in Chap. 1) was an important element of public credit flowing to Greece.

This is also confirmed by Fig. 6.2. For a selected group of euro countries, this figure shows the developments of aggregate (private and public) consumption relative to net national income. While most countries were persistently below the 100% level, Greece and Portugal hovered way above this level up to this writing. Prominent economists from all over the world, including Nobel prize winners Krugman (2015) and Stiglitz (2014), called this "austerity".

---

[13] Note that financing the current account deficit logically does not mean causing it and creating correlations; this is a straw man statement that some critics have blamed on the author.

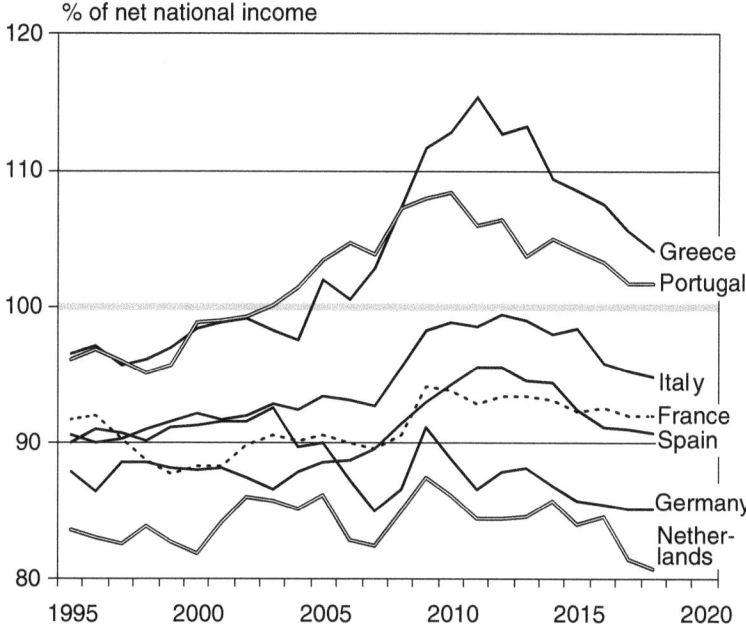

Fig. 6.2 Aggregate public and private consumption in relation to net national income. (Sources: Eurostat, Database, Economy and finance, National accounts (ESA 2010), Annual national accounts, Main GDP aggregates, GDP and main components; Eurostat, Database, Economy and finance, National accounts (ESA 2010), Annual national accounts, Annual sector accounts (ESA 2010), Non-financial transactions)

CHAPTER 7

External and Internal Money

If a country's sum of Target and cash balances is positive, external liquidity must have flown in. This external liquidity fulfils functions similar to internal liquidity which has resulted from the local NCB's purchases of assets and provision of refinancing credits to commercial banks. However it originates from money creation and lending activities of other NCBs. This is the reason why the local NCB is allocated compensating Target and cash balance claims on the Eurosystem. In some northern Eurozone countries, in 2012 and 2013 the external money as measured by the balances crowded out most of the internal money. In Germany and Finland, the crowding out was actually 100%.

7.1 Some Definitions and Identities

As already explained, the Target balances in the first phase of the crisis up to 2012 were generated by the asymmetry in the lending of base money by the NCBs. For the calculation of the interest on the balances, which will be discussed in Chap. 9, and to generally understand the issue, it is important to clarify what the financial institutions in the recipient countries have done with the inflowing liquidity. During this first phase, they did not primarily use liquidity to replenish their liquidity buffers but to return existing central bank money that they had borrowed from their NCBs. This meant that they could save interest expenses, or, if they instead used the money to replenish time deposits with the NCB, that they could earn interest. Investing the incoming liquidity in time deposits has a similar negative liquidity effect as the repayment of refinancing credit. Both lower the local monetary base.

To be more specific, the NCBs of the south lent out over-proportionate amounts of base money to local banks, and the surplus money went to the north for the purchase of goods and assets (including the repayment of foreign debt, which is a repurchase of debt instruments in economic terms). The northern banks in turn used the money to repay existing NCB loans net of time

© The Author(s) 2020
H.-W. Sinn, *The Economics of Target Balances*,
https://doi.org/10.1007/978-3-030-50170-9_7

deposits held with these NCBs. Thus, effectively money creation loans were transferred from the north to the south of the euro area.[1]

"External money" is what I call the money circulated in a country by way of international payment orders and the cash flowing in physically from abroad, because it stemmed from foreign refinancing and foreign open market operations. By contrast, the money created by the domestic NCB's refinancing loans and open market operations, net of time deposits (which are not counted as part of the country's monetary base) I call "internal money". When issuing internal money, an NCB acquires a security or a claim against a private commercial bank on its territory. External money, however, results in a positive Target and cash balance, and instead of acquiring a security or a claim against a commercial bank, the NCB acquires a claim against the Eurosystem which itself builds up a corresponding claim against NCBs with negative cash and Target balances.

A look at some definitions and identities linking the relevant monetary policy aggregates is very important in order to clarify the difference between these two origins of a country's base money in a currency union.

The stock of base money issued by NCB i (and not base money circulating in country i) consists of cash B_i, minimum reserves M_i and excess liquidity U_i. This stock came about either by way of payment orders as measured by the Target balances T_i or by an excess of the stock of "monetary assets" or "money creation credit" (refinancing loans and securities purchased) A_i above the term deposits L_i:

$$T_i + A_i - L_i \equiv B_i + M_i + U_i. \tag{7.1}$$

In addition, cash coming in physically from abroad may be circulating in economy i. As explained in Chap. 3, the latter is assumed in the Eurosystem to be measured by the cash balance

$$S_i \equiv \bar{B}_i - B_i, \tag{7.2}$$

where $\bar{B}_i$ is the statutory stock of money balances which is proportional to the stock of paid-in equity capital and hence roughly proportional to a country's size. Using (7.2), it is possible to rewrite Eq. (7.1) as

$$G_i = \underbrace{T_i + S_i}_{\text{External money}} + \underbrace{A_i - L_i}_{\text{Internal money}}. \tag{7.3}$$

where

---

[1] Sinn and Wollmershäuser (2011, 2012), Homburg (2011, 2012), Sinn (2011c, 2012a, 2014a, 2015b).

7 EXTERNAL AND INTERNAL MONEY

$$G_i \equiv \overline{B}_i + M_i + U_i \qquad (7.4)$$

is the monetary base of country i. Equation (7.3) is the "fundamental accounting identity" used in this book. It separates the national monetary base of country i into external and internal money, that is on the one hand the money that is measured by the Target and cash balances, and on the other hand the money that results from refinancing loans and open market purchases net of an NCB's time deposits. Note that time deposits do not count as part of the monetary base in the Eurozone.

7.2 EXTERNAL MONEY CROWDS OUT INTERNAL MONEY: THE CASE OF GERMANY

Figure 7.1 reveals the magnitudes of the two kinds of base money in the Eurozone's biggest economy, Germany. In the first years of the euro crisis, until about 2013, a great deal of foreign money landed in Germany, although the explosion in Target balances in this period (see Figs. 1.1 and 5.1) also went along with a cash outflow that augmented the Bundesbank's negative cash balance. The external money increased the reserves of the banks, but at the same time it displaced the internal money because the banks repaid their expensive refinancing loans or made (interest-bearing) time deposits with the Bundesbank. Already in the spring of 2011, the payment orders rose so quickly that it was foreseeable that the internal money would be completely displaced, and such a complete displacement actually occurred shortly thereafter. Figure 7.1 illustrates how this comes about.

The topmost curve in Fig. 7.1 shows the Bundesbank's own base money issued. The double curve below shows the German monetary base adjusted for the physical cash outflows. The bottom curve shows the internal money circulating in Germany. The difference between the monetary base and the internal money is the external money. It can be seen that the amount of external money in 2012 and 2013 comprised the entire monetary base, while the internal money issued by the Bundesbank by way of credit operations was completely displaced. At that time, there was no longer any money in Germany that the Bundesbank had put into circulation by way of credit operations with the German banking sector including open market operations. Interestingly, the same situation prevailed in Finland.[2] In the meantime, however, the amount of internal money has risen again because, on the one hand, the huge QE program was set up, which forced every NCB, including the Bundesbank, to inject new internal money into the circuit, while on the other hand the possibility of shifting this money to interest-bearing time deposits was eliminated in mid-2014.

---

[2] See Sinn (2015b, p. 267, figure 6.8).

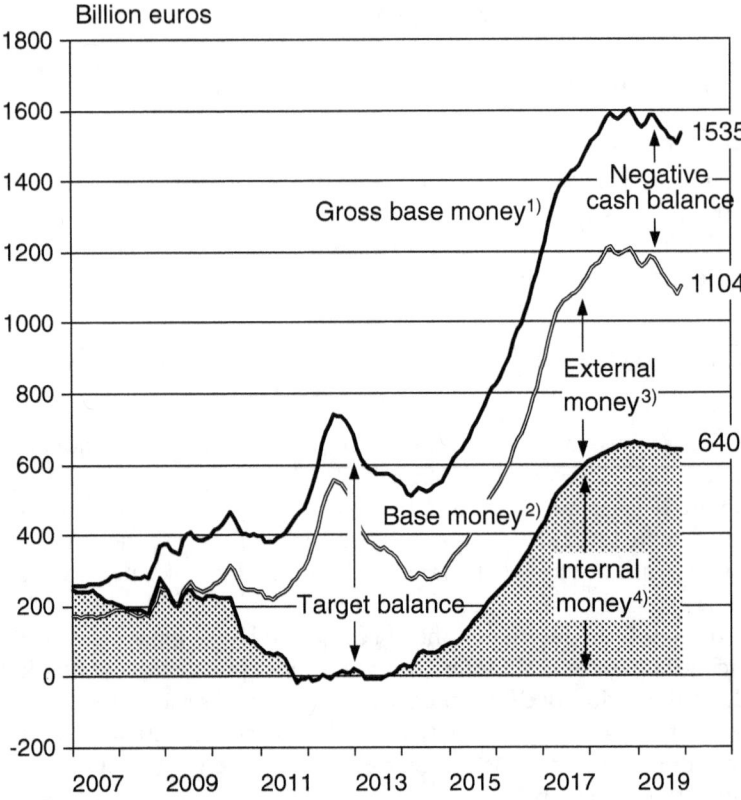

Fig. 7.1 Internal money, external money, and the total stock of base money in Germany. (Sources: Deutsche Bundesbank Eurosystem unter Statistiken, Zeitreihen-Datenbanken: Außenwirtschaft, Zeitreihen, Auslandsposition der Deutschen Bundesbank und Banken und andere finanzielle Unternehmen, Banken, Bankstatistische Gesamtrechnungen, Bankstatistische Gesamtrechnungen in der Europäischen Währungsunion, Liquiditätsposition des Bankensystems, available online at https://www.bundesbank.de/de/statistiken/zeitreihen-datenbanken. Notes: The curves show moving three-month-averages. (1) Gross base money = internal money + Target balance. (2) Monetary base = gross base money + cash balance = internal money + external money. (3) External money = Target balance + cash balance. (4) Internal money = refinancing loans—term deposits of commercial banks with Bundesbank + assets owned by Bundesbank at historical purchasing costs)

CHAPTER 8

The QE Program and the Target balances

The ECB's QE program carried out during the years 2015 to 2018, which increased the Eurozone's stock of central bank money from 1.2 trillion to 3.2 trillion euros, involved a purchase of public sector bonds worth 2.1 billion euros in the Public Sector Purchasing Programme. The program effectively rescheduled the external public debt of countries like Italy and Spain by replacing securitized government debt in the hands of international private investors with mere Target debt of their respective NCBs. As the sellers typically used the sales proceeds to reinvest them in Germany, Germany's Target balances increased strongly despite the symmetry of the NCB's purchases.

8.1 A Liquidity Flood Named QE

With the Quantitative Easing (QE), the third crisis phase, as shown in Fig. 5.1, began. This phase followed the relaxation phase (II), which was initiated by the OMT program ("whatever it takes") and the permanent rescue program ESM. Because the Target balances increased again explosively in this phase, it is useful to discuss the relationship between the Target balances and QE in detail.

As part of the QE program, also known as the Asset Purchasing Program (APP), securities were purchased for €2.6 trillion in the period from autumn 2014 to the end of 2018,[1] i.e. in just four years, of which in conflict with Article 123 TFEU (prohibition of direct government financing by the Eurosystem) €2.1 trillion were issued by public institutions (Public Sector Purchasing Programme, PSPP).[2] Of these, around €1.9 billion were purchases

---

[1] Hammermann et al. (2019).

[2] European Central Bank (2019a). The German Constitutional Court (Bundesverfassungsgericht 2014, 2017) expressed severe doubts about the conformity of the OMT decision with the Maastricht Treaty on the grounds that it might have violated Germany's authority over its government budget and asked the European Court of Justice for a ruling. However, the European Court

© The Author(s) 2020
H.-W. Sinn, *The Economics of Target Balances*,
https://doi.org/10.1007/978-3-030-50170-9_8

of genuine government bonds by the NCBS. The remainder included purchases of bonds issued by the European rescue funds and the European Investment Bank. And in addition to the NCBs, the ECB itself participated in the purchases. The rest of the €2.6 trillion is mainly explained by various forms of private securities. The Eurosystem's base money supply rose from these and complementary measures such as Longer Term Refinancing Operations (LTROs) within just four years from €1.2 trillion at the end of 2014 to around €3.2 trillion at the end of 2018.

The lion's share of the PSPP envisaged a symmetrical issue of base money by means of the open market policy in the sense that each NCB bought the government bonds of "their" state in proportion to the size of the country (paid-in capital share). As, unlike the first phase of the crisis, there was no longer any asymmetrical lending and injection of liquidity by the NCBs, Target balances could not really be expected. And yet this program led to a new boost in the development of the balances. From summer 2014, in anticipation of the expected QE program, there was a trend reversal in the balances that had previously decreased due to the OMT program and the ESM in 2012. The German Target balance increased to €895 billion euros by the end of 2019, Finland's to €57 billion and The Netherland's to €46 billion, while Italy's fell to—€439 billion and Spain's to—€392 billion (see Figs. 5.1 and 7.1) including the references given there).

So much surplus liquidity was created everywhere that one could transfer much of it to Germany, Finland and the Netherlands without fear of drying up the local stock of money balances in circulation. The absolute amount of foreign currency that had flown to Germany—that is, the difference of German Target claims and cash liabilities—increased dramatically, and it shot the monetary base up, as Fig. 7.1 showed already. By the end of 2019, the stock of German base money was more than five times as large as in 2007, shortly before the start of the euro crisis.

8.2 The Great Debt Restructuring

Opinions about the new rise in Target balances having been linked to QE are mixed. While the European Central Bank (2016e, pp. 22f.) sees this rise as a natural reaction of the markets developing around Frankfurt and not an expression of "stress factors" in the Eurosystem, as in the period before the summer of 2012, Westermann (2016a, b) describes it as an implicit wave of new capital flight. The evidence, in his opinion, lies in the fact that the money stayed in Germany and other countries of the north or was transferred there. He posed the rhetorical question of whether the money would have stayed in Rome, Lisbon or Athens if it had ended up there for natural reasons.

---

of Justice (2015, 2018) subsequently dismissed these doubts and ruled that the ECB had acted in line with the EU treaties. A new opinion, or even a ruling, of the German Court on these issues is expected in May 2020, after the completion of this manuscript.

An alternative way of explaining why the symmetrical repurchase of government bonds could imply such a huge rise in Target balances is simply that an over-proportional part of the government bonds of the southern Eurozone countries was lying in portfolios outside these countries, because they had issued them in the past to finance their chronic current account deficits, which prevailed not only during the first few years of the euro but even before the euro was introduced. Thus the symmetrical repurchases by the national NCBs automatically meant net payment orders to other countries that implied rising Target liabilities at home and rising Target claims there. And unless the foreign investors had actively tried to re-channel the funds they received back to the issuing countries to buy other assets there, these Target imbalances would have persisted.

Whatever the truth, the renewed rise in the balances definitely implies an act of debt rescheduling, by which southern marketable securitized sovereign debt was converted to mere Target debt (Sinn 2016a, pp. 247–53, 2016b, 2018b, c). With the repurchase of government bonds by the NCBs, government bonds held in the portfolios of private investors, who in the case of default could become very disagreeable, were returned to government institutions belonging to the states that had issued them. The debt rescheduling eliminated this form of sovereign debt and transformed private financing of previous government expenditure into subsequent financing by other NCBs and hence to creditors who in a crisis would be less nasty than private investors and who could be manipulated politically.

The tension between this process and Article 123 TFEU, which prohibits the direct financing of states with central bank loans, is evident, and it is particularly great when the financing is a completely natural, predictable effect, as the ECB claims, rather than the result of stress factors.

The new increase of the Target balances came about when the NCBs bought government bonds from private investors wherever they were located—at home, in other euro countries or non-euro countries. The private investors typically did not hold the money they received but used it to also rebalance their portfolios, initiating a sequence of portfolio reshuffling involving many different types of investors and countries.

Strictly speaking, the new Target balances even came about somewhat earlier, from summer 2014 (see Fig. 5.1), because investors anticipated the purchases and expected profitable arbitrage opportunities. Italian investors in particular had already started buying securities internationally in the summer and autumn of 2014, driving up the Italian Target debt.[3]

---

[3] See Figs. 5.1 and 8.1 which follows below. Early purchases also were made easier because the ECB launched a new program of Targeted Longer Term Refinancing Operations (TLTROs) in June 2014, which replaced the previous programs and provided advance liquidity that clever banks used to buy government bonds in the market, expecting that they would soon be able to resell them to the NCBs of the Eurozone. The banks in Italy were heavily involved in the new TLTRO program, using a third of the available funds, even though Italy's economy accounts only for a

In the end, a disproportionate portion of the liquidity injected through the QE sales flowed to Germany. The liquidity was used for private debt redemption and to acquire government bonds, stocks, real estate and many other assets. The net payment orders involved caused the German Target balances to rise dramatically.

The fact that big foreign banks were able to fill and file demand deposits with the Bundesbank also contributed to the balances. However, this was only a transitory and ultimately small item—at the end of 2018 a mere 54 billion euros.[4]

The new Target balances were not only due to private portfolio reallocations. Part of them also came about because foreign NCBs repurchased the domestic government bonds from investors in Germany and gave direct payment orders to the Bundesbank. For example, the Banco de España was able to instruct the Bundesbank to create new money and give it to a German life insurer so that the life insurer could return its Spanish government bonds to the Banco de España, an institution owned by the Spanish state. The life insurer received book money for this, that is a claim against a German commercial bank, and the bank itself was paid by the Bundesbank with newly created base money, which enters as a liability in the Bundesbank balance sheet. The Bundesbank, in turn, received a Target claim against the Eurosystem to compensate for crediting the business, and the Eurosystem received a claim against the Banco de España.

The life insurer was then likely to have used his money to buy other interest-bearing assets, so that someone else became the money holder in its place. It probably only shifted its portfolio from the Spanish government bonds to other interest-bearing investments. If the second seller, that is, the one who sold these other assets to the German life insurer, lived outside of Germany, the effect on the Target balances neutralized until other investors in the chain of portfolio reshufflings eventually again invested in Germany.

Benoit Coeuré (2017), board member of the ECB, reports that a lot of the proceeds from the first round of government bond repurchases under the QE program went to US government bonds. Investors typically remained in the same asset class and only changed the country of issue. But of course the euros used for the purchases did not stay in the US, because there was no need for more euro transactions cash, but flowed back for investments into the euro area, primarily to Germany. Here, the Target balances grew at an exorbitant rate, much more than in all other countries such as Luxembourg and the Netherlands, where there was also significant growth.

In Germany, part of the money will initially have flowed into bank accounts. However, since the chain of portfolio reallocations initiated by the QE

---

seventh of the economy of the Eurozone. See European Central Bank (2019b, p. 41) and Banca d'Italia (2019, p. 28).

[4] Deutsche Bundesbank (2019, p. 62) in connection with a letter of the Bundesbank to the author of 4 September 2019.

program mostly concerned professional investment companies, it can be assumed that this was only a transitory effect and that a substantial part of the funds was ultimately reinvested in interest-bearing investment properties. The huge boom in German real estate and stocks in recent years certainly suggests this. In essence, the German sellers will now probably be the money holders, as will those citizens who no longer dare to invest their savings out of current income other than in the form of bank accounts and cash, given the fact that asset prices are very high already. However, this is more dangerous than the citizens may realize, because the plans to devalue money through inflation and negative deposit interest rates, as well as in the form of a direct devaluation of physical in relation to electronic central bank money, which eventually would be the only legal tender, are already on the table under the name of "dual currency.[5]

8.3 The Example of Italy

Clear indications that the additional liquidity created in the course of the asset purchases did not just end up in deposits held by the sellers of government assets but was invested in other profitable assets can be found in the 2017 annual report of Banca d'Italia (2018, pp. 128f), which summarizes its findings as follows:

> [...] the increase in Italy's TARGET2 debtor position in the first two years of the APP was mainly offset by the foreign securities purchases by Italian residents ... This reflects a portfolio shift from government securities and bank bonds towards domestic and foreign asset management and insurance products, displaying greater international diversification. The APP contributed to the rebalancing of residents' portfolios [...]

This statement confirms the above interpretation that QE was essentially a portfolio reallocation in the course of which domestic government bonds in the investors' portfolios were replaced by interest-bearing assets from other countries.

The portfolio reallocation was a reflection of the rescheduling of Italian debt, that is, the fact that Italy was able to replace its government debt to the private sector with the Target debt of the Banca d'Italia to the Eurosystem. This debt rescheduling benefited the Italian state and enabled Italian investors to save their wealth and transfer it to safe havens. Figure 8.1, which contains a subset of the information provided in a complex double graph of the Banca d'Italia, which is entitled "Main factors influencing the Target2 balances", illustrates the facts. Obviously, in the period up to mid-2014, the path of the rising and declining Target debt in Italy was very closely correlated with the stock of refinancing loans that the Banca d'Italia had issued. This corresponds

---

[5] See Assenmacher and Krogstrup (2018).

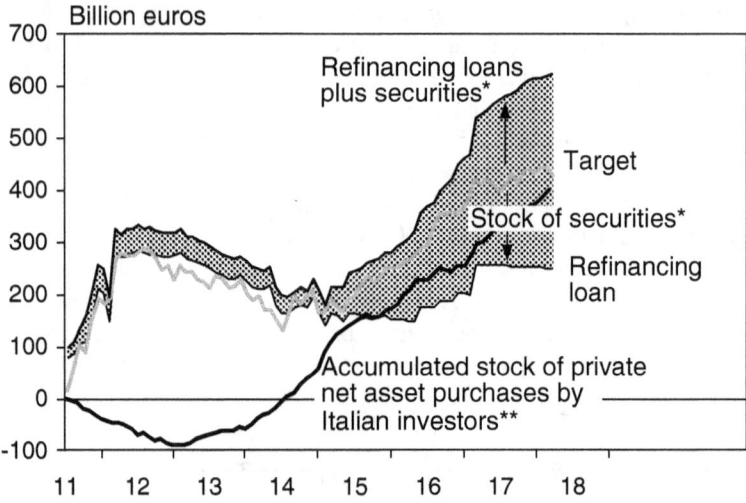

Fig. 8.1 Stocks of bonds and refinancing loans of Banca d'Italia as well as foreign securities owned by Italians in relation to the Italian Target debt. *Banca d'Italia's stock of securities for monetary policy purposes (without ANFA). **Accumulation since 1 July 2011. (Source: Banca d'Italia (2018, p. 128). Notes: This graph shows a newly designed excerpt from a double figure of the Banca d'Italia with the heading "Main Factors Influencing the Target Balances". It begins, like the original figure, in July 2011, when the Italian crisis broke out, the Eurosystem NCBs began to buy Italian government bonds under the SMP, and Italy's Target balances nonetheless changed signs, becoming increasingly negative (cf. Fig. 5.1). The graph ends, as the original does, in April 2018 (or March 2018 for the curve of Italian net asset purchases abroad))

to the analysis of Chap. 5, but only up to this point. From summer 2014, the anticipated and then realized security purchases in Italy as part of the QE program became an alternative source of liquidity, which implied that the path of refinancing loans distanced itself from the path of Target credit. The overall increase in liquidity weakened the relationship between Target debt and money creation credit in general because only a portion of it was used for payment orders to other countries. Italian investors took the opportunity to sell Italian government bonds to Banca d'Italia and used the revenues to buy other securities abroad, that is to reschedule their securities, as was explained above. A disproportionate portion of the new base money that came into circulation through the Italian APP eventually ended up in Germany through further international portfolio shifts, for otherwise the German Target balances could not have increased so dramatically.

The Italian government has been able to use the QE program to shift its outstanding debt held by private investors to its own central bank, as it had regularly done before the euro. In this respect, it continued with established traditions. However, it now replaced its securitized debt to private investors with mere Target debt to the Eurosystem and ultimately, indirectly, mainly to the Bundesbank. This gives the process a new, more piquant note.

8.4 Triangular Transactions with Investors Outside the Eurozone

The triangular transactions of the Eurozone's NCBs with investors from all over the world in the course of the QE program are even more unsettling.[6] For example, an investor from Hong Kong was able to sell his Spanish government bonds for euros to the Spanish NCB and then invest the proceeds of the sale in Germany by acquiring shares in a German company. In the end, the Spanish government paper came back into the hands of an institution owned by the Spanish state, and in return the Chinese investor had been given title to the German company. The German seller of the company in turn received book money, i.e. a claim against a German bank, which was itself offset by a deposit claim against the Bundesbank. The Bundesbank was compensated with a claim against the Eurosystem, while the Banco de España built up a corresponding debt towards this system.

Such triangular transactions were, as the ECB then reported, of considerable importance. According to Coeuré (2017), 45 percent of the securities acquired by the Eurosystem NCBs were sold by non-euro area investors, and these investors then reinvested the sales proceeds primarily in equity issued in the euro area.

The strong devaluation that the euro has experienced since the summer of 2014 at the same time as the new build-up of the German Target balances due to speculative transactions speaks for the importance of triangular transactions. The buybacks of European government bonds from the portfolios of investors around the world meant a massive supply of euros on the currency markets, which generated speculative devaluation effects even before the actual event. At a falling euro exchange rate, the European NCBs managed to buy their respective government bonds around the world, and the falling exchange rate made it attractive for foreign investors to subsequently invest the sales proceeds in European company shares. The particular interest of investors was Germany, whose company shares, at least initially, were able to shine with favorable price-earnings ratios.

Chinese buyers stood out among the buyers of German corporate assets, and not only because some spectacular purchases made headlines. In terms of euros spent, Chinese purchases of European corporate holdings in 2016 were more than four times as large as in 2014. After that, they eased somewhat because the best cherries had been picked. Germany clearly headed the list of the reported euro countries for Chinese corporate asset purchases.[7]

---
[6] See Westermann (2016a, b), and Sinn (2016a since second edition, pp. 211f. and pp. 263f., 2016b).
[7] See Berchtold and Sun (2019).

Whether a debt rescheduling action or a technical effect; the new increase in Target balances as a result of the QE program is highly questionable from a German perspective, because the Bundesbank was twice driven into a conflict with the Maastricht Treaty.[8] On the one hand, with its part of the program, i.e. the purchase of German government bonds, it had to retroactively finance the German state, which contradicts the objective of Article 123 TFEU (prohibition of monetary government funding). On the other hand, it also had to participate indirectly in the retroactive financing of other states by carrying out and crediting the payment orders to Germany resulting from the repurchase of government bonds. The debate as to whether it was good that the QE program ultimately ensured that the debt relief of European countries also came about by replacing European government bonds that Chinese investors returned to their countries of origin with ownership titles in European companies remains to be seen—also against the background of new legislation enacted by the European Parliament to make it more difficult for investors from non-EU countries to buy European companies in strategically important areas of the economy.[9]

It must also be discussed whether the Bundesbank's Target claims represent an adequate substitute for the company shares provided from an economic point of view—or whether these are uncertain claims that put the German taxpayer at risk. The private investors and owners from various countries that were involved must all have made their deals, otherwise they would not have participated. Chapter 12 will discuss this in more detail.

---

[8] The president of the Bundesbank, Jens Weidmann, abstained from voting in favor of the QE program according to information revealed by Reuters (2019).

[9] See European Parliament (2019). Cf. also Bundesministerium für Wirtschaft und Energie (2018) as well as Doll and Kaiser (2018).

CHAPTER 9

The Effective Rate of Interest on Target Balances

According to formal decisions of the ECB's Governing Council, Target and cash balances carry a rate of interest equal to the ECB's main refinancing rate. However, the Council also decided that all primary interest income of the NCBs is pooled and redistributed according to country size. The pooling eliminates the statutory interest on the balances, but at the same time it implies an effective rate of intra-Eurosystem interest on them, given that the balances measure international liquidity flows that cause changes in the primary interest incomes collected by the NCBs, which is neutralized by pooling. The effective rate of interest on the balances is a weighted average of the ECB's policy interest rates where the weights are determined by the structure of the sources and sinks of international liquidity flows that are measured by the Target balances. As the intra-Eurosystem interest payments are booked as additional Target balances and imply secondary liquidity flows from the Target debtor to the Target creditor economies, pooling actually implies compound interest. Usually, the effective rate of interest is positive, but with the ECB's current set of policy interest rates, its sign has turned negative.

9.1 Why the Interest Problem Is Relevant

As Target and cash balances, which result from electronic and physical payments across country boundaries, qualify as credits or loans among the NCBs of the Eurozone, as was explained in Chaps. 2 and 4, a natural question is whether, and if so, what rate of interest they bear.

The interest issue may seem unimportant in a world where many policy interest rates are zero or even negative. Yet, for one, they will probably not stay that low forever, and for another, negative rates do have important redistributive implications as well. This chapter will discuss the general question of whether the Target and cash balances bear interest in principle and derive general algebraic equations that would hold both for positive and negative rates. The topic is also relevant, because, if the balances did not bear interest in principle, one might well argue that fair value accounting implies that they such should not enter the official balance sheets of the NCBs, as they do.[1] (Recall the analysis of Chap. 3 on this issue.) This view might be countered on the grounds that NCBs do not use fair value accounting anyway, but historical cost accounting.[2] Yet, when it comes to an assessment of potential economic risks involved with the credit measured by the balances, fair value accounting would certainly be more appropriate than historical cost accounting. After all, the balances originate from transactions, by which goods and assets were given away. If these goods and assets were gone without the surplus country ever getting anything back, that would be a major redistribution of real resources among the countries of the Eurozone that, once realized, could trigger opposition to the euro project as such, if not the entire European unification process. It would also be a problem for the surplus country if it had to wait for an indefinite distant future at best, without getting compound interest or if the interest return on the delivery of goods and assets financed by intra-Eurosystem credit would be subject to bankruptcy risks, an issue that will be discussed in Chap. 12.

9.2 Legal Provisions for Intra-Eurosystem Interest Payments

In view of these problems, it is comforting at first glance that there are a number of provisions in the statutes and bylaws of the Eurosystem that provide evidence of interest on the balances actually being paid or, at least, evidence of the intention of doing so. As was cited already in Chap. 3, the ECB's accounting rules require the "remuneration of TARGET2 balances" to be booked in a country's "current account", which is a subset of its balance of payments statistics.[3] For one, this statement unambiguously clarifies that there is the intention and expectation to have interest on Target balances being paid after all. For another, it stipulates that intra-Eurosystem interest payments should be treated in the same way as international interest flows between private institutions.

Moreover, the Bundesbank, in accord with the ECB, cited an unpublished decision in a letter to the Ifo Institute according to which the NCBs pay interest to one another according to their Target and cash balances:[4]

> Intra-Eurosystem balances [...] are remunerated at the latest available marginal interest rate used by the Eurosystem in its tenders for main refinancing operations ...

---

[1] Cf. Hellwig (2018b, pp. 363 and 377).

[2] See European Central Bank (2012a, pp. 87–98). The NCBs chose this accounting method, as they wanted to inform more about their monetary policy than about the true value of their assets. Scholze and Westermann (2014) therefore propose simultaneously using two separate accounting systems.

[3] European Central Bank (2016f., no. 3.10.4, p. 59; see also no. 3.10.3, p. 58).

[4] Unpublished decision ECB/2007/NP10 on interest yield of intra-Eurosystem net balances, article 2, paragraph 1, revealed to the author by the Bundesbank, in consent with the ECB: Bundesbank, answer No. 2011/003864 to a letter of the Ifo Institute of 11 March 2011. A related letter of the ECB was sent to the Ifo Institute on 15 March 2012. Moreover, one day after the first publication on the issue of rising Target balances (Sinn 2011a, 21 February) the author was informed in an email note by the ECB chief economist that the Target balances do bear interest.

This decision is implicitly confirmed by European Central Bank (2016g, Annex I, 6) in a somewhat different context (pooling):[5]

> Net intra-Eurosystem liabilities resulting from TARGET2 transactions (are) remunerated at the reference rate.

9.3 Pooling: A Comprehensive Way of Calculating Intra-Eurosystem Interest on Target and Cash Balances

However, the provisions written down in the statutes and accounting manuals apply to sub-year and preliminary intra-Eurosystem interest payments[6] and are part of a more comprehensive and complicated calculation in the Eurosystem's interest mechanism which takes place by the end of the year and may overrule the preliminary payments as cited. This final calculation results from the fact that, in addition to the cited provisions for the payment of intra-Eurosystem interest, the European Central Bank (2001, preamble 2; 2016g, preamble 3) decided that all interest income that NCBs earn from monetary policy operations is to be pooled in the Eurozone and redistributed in proportion to the respective countries' paid-in capital keys, that is roughly in proportion to country size.[7] As has been pointed out by number of authors,[8] pooling implies that the distribution of interest income among the NCBs is independent of where the interest income is generated.

Some scholars have suspected that this implies that there is no intra-Eurosystem interest on the Target and cash balances.[9] However, this conclusion is too hasty because, in fact, pooling is the decisive mechanism through which intra-Eurosystem interest on Target and cash balances are calculated and come about. Why this is so will be explained intuitively below, and formally in the next two sections of this chapter.

To clarify what pooling means and to simplify the discussion, let us assume for a while that all policy interest rates are strictly positive, i.e. that a national NCB pays positive deposit rates on term deposits, demand deposits and

---

[5] An early notice of the calculation of Intra-Eurosystem interest was given by the European Central Bank (2001, preamble, paragraph 7), which states: "The net balance of the intra-Eurosystem claims and liabilities on euro banknotes in circulation should be remunerated by applying an objective criterion defining the cost of money. In this context, the main refinancing operations rate used by the Eurosystem in its tenders for main refinancing operations is regarded as appropriate." However, this does not mention the Target balances, which were not an issue at the time, given that the implicit initial assumption was that the balances should be always kept close to zero. See former Bundesbank president Schlesinger (2012) who reported that Target "originally was only supposed to be a clearing system without lending".

[6] European Central Bank (2016g, article 2.3).

[7] See Chap. 4. While the ECB published some fundamentals of the pooling process, not all relevant aspects of the calculation process have been revealed. For further important details concerning the pooling of ELA, ANFA and PSPP risks see Box 9.1 below.

[8] In the sequence of publication dates, Sinn (2014a, p. 179, 2015b, p. 254, 2018c, pp. 32–34, 2018d), van Suntum (2018), Fuest and Sinn (2018a, b), Hellwig (2018b).

[9] See Hellwig (2018b) as well as Hellwig and Schnabel (2019). The analysis offered by these authors was rejected in a comment by Sinn (2019b).

minimum reserves that commercial banks sustain with it. Assume moreover that it collects an even higher refinancing rate on its money creation credit (refinancing credit and assets purchased). Below and above-normal interest on ELA, ANFA and PSPP assets are not part of the pooling process for reasons explained in Box 9.1 and are therefore not considered here. Let us call the NCB's interest paid to, or coming from, the non-central bank sector *primary interest* as opposed to *secondary interest* measuring an NCB's interest income after pooling and intra-Eurosystem redistribution of seignorage income. The terms "primary" and "secondary" income are similar to those used in Public Finance to compare the income distribution among citizens before and after the government's redistribution measures. Boxes 9.1 and 9.2 clarify and specify the assumptions about the policy interest rates in more detail empirically. The assumption of positive policy rates will be relaxed in Sect. 9.5.

The difference between an NCB's primary interest revenue and its primary interest expenses is its *primary seignorage income*. It is assumed that the policy interest rates are chosen such that the primary seignorage income would be strictly positive in the absence of Target and cash balances and when there are no defaults. (Chap. 12 elaborates on the latter assumption.) Adding intra-Eurosystem interest payments resulting from the pooling process generates the NCB's *secondary seignorage income* which is distributed to the government budget.

For the pooling process and the redistribution of interest income, which is completed by the end of every year, it does not matter who delivers the primary seignorage income to the pool that a debtor NCB earns from its contacts with other sectors of the economy—the NCB itself or the Target and cash balance creditors who receive the prior intra-Eurosystem interest payments resulting from the ECB's statutes as described in the previous section. Thus, the pre-payment is an ultimately meaningless intermediate step in the pooling calculations similar to the pre-payment of taxes on wage income which in many economies is taken into account, and overruled, by the end-of-year income tax declaration.

The important point to understand is that pooling and redistribution of primary interest income implies an effective intra-Eurosystem interest on the Target and cash balances. For one, the balances measure an international transfer in liquidity between countries that causes an international reallocation in the primary seignorage incomes earned by the NCBs, because the transfer of liquidity empties a source and fills a sink which both generate interest incomes for the NCBs. For another, pooling implies that secondary seignorage incomes are independent of the Target and cash balances. If follows that pooling induces a compensating intra-Eurosystem seignorage flow whose magnitude is directly related to, and caused by, the Target and cash balances.

The intra-Eurosystem reallocation of seignorage through pooling is recorded as additional Target claims and liabilities in the respective balance sheets. This follows from the Target2 guidelines of the European Central Bank (2012b, article 5) which state:[10]

---

[10] The correctness of this interpretation of the article was confirmed to the author in an exchange with Deutsche Bundesbank, letters of 11 and 17 March 2020. A corresponding statement that, however, only refers to the interest on cash balances can be found in European Central Bank (2001, article 2, paragraph 3; 2016g, article 2, paragraph 3).

Intra-European System of Central Banks (ESCB) transactions shall be processed through TARGET2...

Accordingly, the recipient creditor NCB builds up a further Target claim and the paying debtor NCB a further Target liability. However, the reallocation of seignorage is more than just an accounting issue. It extracts liquidity and income from the debtor country and injects it into the economy of the creditor country, because the NCB's customers in the former pay more and in the latter less interest in net terms. The repercussions for the capital market equilibrium and market interest rates resulting from this liquidity flow will be discussed towards the end of this chapter and in Chap. 10.

To be more specific, assume that there were international liquidity flows by way of payment orders between just two countries of the Eurosystem, building up mirrored non-zero Target balances in the first place. Disregard for a moment the possibility of changing the amounts of bank notes issued. The NCB of the source country attains a debtor position, and the NCB of the sink country a creditor position. The transfer of liquidity with necessity means that the debtor NCB has to pay primary interest on a smaller volume of deposits or earns primary interest from a larger stock of money creation credit. Thus, the NCB's overall primary seignorage income extracted from the non-central bank sector rises.

Without pooling, the debtor NCB's additional primary seignorage income resulting from the Target liability would be distributed to the member state, which would use it to finance its budget. Given the state's expenses, local tax payers would ultimately benefit from the extra primary seignorage income resulting from the Target liability, and the liquidity withdrawn from the national economy by way of collecting primary seignorage would be fully channeled back to it. Both the primary seignorage income and the liquidity that the NCB is able to collect because of the Target balance stay at home while goods and assets had been imported upon building up the Target balance.

With pooling, this is not the case, however, because the debtor NCB cannot distribute its extra primary seignorage profit to the state, but must transfer it to the pool from where little if anything is returning. Suppose for simplicity that the structures of the sources and sinks of liquidity in the debtor and creditor countries are the same. In this case, nothing is returning as the loss in primary seignorage by the creditor NCB is exactly equal to the extra primary seignorage income collected by the debtor NCB. The Eurosystem's aggregate primary interest income remains constant, and so do secondary seignorage incomes that the NCBs earn after pooling and can distribute to their states. The entire amount of extra primary seignorage that the debtor NCB collects is lost and gained by the creditor NCB.

This has two implications. For one, there are intra-Eurosystem income flows among the NCBs that compensate for their changes in primary seignorage incomes and are recorded in the Target system. As these intra-Eurosystem income flows are caused by the original Target balance and are increasing with the size of this balance, they qualify as effective intra-Eurosystem interest on this original balance. Pooling obviously is an elegant and comprehensive way of calculating and delivering intra-Eurosystem interest on the Target balance.

For another, it follows that the extra interest revenue that the debtor NCB collects because its sources of liquidity were activated—more money creation credit and/or lower deposits—is withdrawn as income *and liquidity* from the domestic economy, but not returned. The return instead takes place in the economy of the creditor NCB where banks pay less interest on money creation credit and more on deposits. In net terms, after pooling, the non-central bank sectors of the debtor economy transfer interest income and liquidity to the non-central bank sectors of the creditor economy. Section 9.7 will elaborate further on this question.

These results also hold if bank notes are included. Suppose the withdrawal of liquidity from the source country by way of payment orders stems from returning bank notes to the local NCB while the extra liquidity arriving in the sink country is used by that country's NCB to issue more bank notes. This would imply that no additional primary interest income is earned by the NCB of the former country and no additional interest income is lost by the NCB of the latter. Hence there would be no redistribution of primary seignorage income and no intra-Eurosystem interest payment. Recall, however, that, as was explained in Chaps. 4 and 7, the statutes of the Eurosystem consider such a reallocation in the amounts of bank notes as a reverse international banknote transfer from the sink to the source country which builds up a negative cash balance in the former and a positive cash balance in the latter. Thus, there would be no change in the sum of each country's Target and cash balances which fits the fact that no intra-Eurosystem interest accrues.

To summarize: The Intra-Eurosystem interest payments on Target and cash balances have implications that in many respects are similar to international interest payments between private debtors and their creditors. They withdraw income and liquidity from the debtors' country and inject income and liquidity into the latter. The similarities justify the cited provision in the Eurosystem's accounting guidelines that the "remuneration of the Target2 balances" has to be booked in a country's "current account" as part of its balance of payments statistics.

A final caveat is appropriate to avoid over-interpreting the result. While the result shows that Target and cash balances effectively bear interest, it is not meant to give a monocausal explanation of intra-Eurosystem redistribution of primary seignorage. Such a redistribution could also emerge, for example, if some countries' commercial banks had an above-normal liquidity preference that they satisfy by borrowing more from their respective NCBs rather than from private creditors in other countries. Given that the NCBs' deposit rates are smaller than the lending rates, this liquidity preference would imply more primary seignorage incomes of these NCBs which are largely "taxed" away by the pooling process. So there would be an international redistribution of primary seignorage without Target and cash balances in this case. The formal approach offered in the next section is not affected by this qualification as it will derive a *marginal* effective rate of (intra-Eurosystem) interest on the Target and cash balances that disregards any intra-marginal effects.

9.4 Primary Seignorage, Secondary Seignorage and the Definition of the Marginal Effective Rate of Interest on Target and Cash Balances

The general considerations of the previous section can be specified more precisely.[11] Let Y_i denote NCB i's *primary seignorage income* to be delivered to the common pool, and X_i the *secondary seignorage income* that NCB i receives from this pool. To repeat: The primary seignorage income is defined as the income that an NCB earns from its contacts with commercial banks and those parts of the economy that do not belong to the European system of central banks, i.e. from refinancing credits to commercial banks, from holding securities issued by private and public institutions and from deposits that commercial banks sustain with the NCB. The secondary interest income is the interest income that is available after redistribution. It is the amount of interest income from monetary policy operations that an NCB can distribute to its respective nation state and that is available as a source of revenue for the local government's budget.[12] Let Z_i be the *redistribution gain* of NCB i, i.e. the excess of the refund from the pool over the contributions to the pool:

$$Z_i \equiv X_i - Y_i. \tag{9.1}$$

NCB i receives the share α_i of the aggregate seignorage income of the pool. As explained above in Chap. 4, α_i is the "paid-in capital key" which is proportional to the average of a country's population and country share.[13] NCB i's secondary seignorage income can therefore be written as

$$X_i = \alpha_i \left(Y_i + Y_{i*} \right), \tag{9.2}$$

where the bracket gives the volume of the pool, that is the aggregate primary seignorage income and Y_{i*} is the sum of all injections of primary seignorage revenue of all NCBs except i into the pool:

$$Y_{i*} \equiv \sum\nolimits_{j=1, j \neq i}^{n} Y_j. \tag{9.3}$$

---

[11] The subsequent specifications largely follow Sinn (2019a).
[12] In addition, there may be a surplus of the return on ANFA assets over the refinancing rate which does not participate in the pooling and may also be distributed to the state. For further details, see Box 9.1.
[13] Recall that, as was explained in Chap. 4, the ECB itself also participates in the Target system and collects 8% of the seignorage, a number which might reflect the euro cash circulating outside the Eurozone as well as Target balances held by associated non-euro countries. The ECB's seignorage revenue after expenses is being distributed to the NCBs. The discussion in the text abstracts from these peculiarities.

It follows from (9.1) and (9.2) that the redistribution gain of NCB i is given by

$$Z_i = \alpha_i Y_{i*} - (1 - \alpha_i) Y_i. \tag{9.4}$$

Thus, an NCB receives from others' primary seignorage income a proportion that is equal to its own magnitude share and gives them all but this proportion of its own primary seignorage income.

The aim of this section is to calculate the marginal effective intra-Eurosystem rate of interest on Target and cash balances according to the definition given above. Formally, the marginal effective rate of interest NCB i earns on its Target and cash balances, $T_i + S_i$, is defined as

$$\rho_i \equiv \frac{dZ_i}{d(T_i + S_i)} \tag{9.5}$$

i.e. as the increase in its redistribution gain caused by a marginal increase in its Target and cash balances.

Assume that NCB i's primary seignorage income is given by

$$Y_i = rA_i - r^L L_i - rM_i - r^U U_i \tag{9.6}$$

which is a combination of the ECB's policy interest rates and various monetary aggregates. The variable r is the main refinancing rate that an NCB earns on its "monetary assets" or "money creation credit" A_i, which is defined as the sum of refinancing loans given to banks and securities purchased. M_i denotes the commercial banks' minimum reserve as required by the ECB. In the Eurosystem the minimum reserve is remunerated at the main refinancing rate r. Moreover, r^L is the term deposit rate that banks can earn on their stock of term deposits L_i held with the NCB and r^U is the deposit facility rate applying to excess liquidity U_i, that is demand deposits banks hold with the NCB beyond the minimum reserve. A justification and discussion of these specifications of the relevant policy interest rates is given in Boxes 9.1 and 9.2 below.

To calculate the effective marginal rate of interest on the Target and cash balances as defined in (9.5), it is important to understand how Target and cash balances affect the monetary aggregates on the right-hand side of (9.6). For this, recall the fundamental accounting identity (7.3) from Chap. 7 which is represented here in a slightly different form, using the definition of country i's monetary base G_i as was given in equation (7.7):

$$T_i + S_i = G_i + L_i - A_i, \quad G_i \equiv \bar{B}_i + M_i + U_i. \tag{9.7}$$

Box 9.1 The rate of return on monetary assets officially assumed for the pooling process

Equation (9.6) is a simplification, abstracting from the fact that some of the assets captured by A_i earn a rate of interest different from r. For example, gold is assumed to bear no interest in the pooling calculations of the Eurosystem. Moreover, Longer Term Refinancing Operations (LTROs) imply funds lent out under conditions tailored to individual bank characteristics.

However, in the statutory standard case in the Eurosystem there is no risk sharing, and in this case the main refinancing rate applies to most assets.[14] As Fuest and Sinn (2015, 2016, 2018a, b) have explained, interest in the amount of the main refinancing rate must normally be transferred to the pool not only for ordinary refinancing loans, but also for ELA and ANFA assets as well as government bonds purchased by NCBs in the Public Sector Purchasing Programme (PSPP), the latter accounting for the largest part of the Eurosystem's monetary base.[15] These assets are purchased at an NCB's own risk, but contrary to a common belief this does not mean that the NCB can collect the entire return and distribute it to its respective state. Instead, it has to pay interest equal to the main refinancing rate into the pool, regardless of whether or not it earns this interest. It can keep any surplus and is liable for any shortcoming of interest earned relative to the main refinancing rate. Even if the respective assets default, the NCB owning them will have to permanently transfer the main refinancing rate of interest on the nominal historical purchasing value of these assets to the pool. As will be shown in Chap. 12, this aspect will be important for the question of whether and when the Target and cash balances do involve a default risk for the other

(*continued*)

---

[14] See article 32.4 of the Protocol (no 4) on the Statute of the European System of Central Banks and of the European Central Bank which reads: "The Governing Council *may decide* that national central banks shall be indemnified against costs incurred in connection with the issue of banknotes or *in exceptional circumstances for specific losses* arising from monetary policy operations undertaken for the ESCB. Indemnification shall be in a form deemed appropriate in the judgment of the Governing Council; these amounts may be offset against the national central banks' monetary income" (italics by the author). Cf. also European Central Bank (2016g, article 3).

[15] In addition, no risk sharing was agreed for some asset purchasing programs such as the first two tranches of the Covered Bond Purchasing programs (CBPP1 and CBPP2). By the end of 2018, the government bonds purchased under the PSPP alone accounted for about €1.9 billion or 60% of the monetary base of the Eurozone (€3.2 billion). (About €0.2 billion of the PSPP were used to buy bonds issued by other public entities such as the intergovernmental rescue programs and the European Investment Bank.) It follows already from this information that only the smaller part of the monetary base came into circulation through monetary policy operations that imply joint liability and risk sharing. Exceptions from the no-risk sharing rule include other bond purchasing programmes

> **Box 9.1 (continued)**
> NCBs and European taxpayers even if no country leaves the Eurosystem.[16] The ECB Council does have the possibility of deviating from this rule and mutualizing the asset risk involved, but this would require a separate decision. This book considers only the normal statutory case.[17]

> **Box 9.2 Why the deposit facility rate can be taken to apply to all excess liquidity**
> Equation (9.6) moreover assumes that the deposit facility rate applies to all excess liquidity. Excess liquidity is the excess of the demand deposits commercial banks hold with the local NCB over the required minimum reserve. As excess liquidity is the sum of what the ECB calls excess reserves and deposit facility, and the deposit facility rate normally applies only to the latter, this may not seem appropriate. However, a distinction between excess reserves and the deposit facility is irrelevant for the purpose of this analysis. Firstly, because banks used to shift their liquidity from the formally interest-free excess reserve to the deposit facility, when the latter was bearing interest. Secondly, because the ECB Council decided on 5 June 2014 to impose the deposit facility rate also on excess reserves, to avoid evasion reactions upon shifting the deposit facility rate into negative territory where it has been up to this writing.[18] Thus, we can assume without any loss of generality that all kinds of demand deposits of banks with their NCBs do indeed bear interest.
>
> The following triple diagram, Fig. 9.1, illustrates the development of the named policy interest rates (upper diagram) and the corresponding stocks of deposits in the Eurosystem since the introduction of the euro. The diagram shows that the relevant interest rates have now become zero or negative, and that term deposits are currently no longer available. It also shows that (lowest diagram) excess reserves were quantitatively negligible when the deposit facility rate was positive and rose sharply when the deposit facility rate became zero, later even negative, and was applied to excess reserves.[19]

(SMP, CBPP3, CSPP), purchases by the ECB itself and refinancing operations other than ELA. For the composition and volume of the purchases see European Central Bank (2019a).

[16] The issue was already clarified in a debate involving Fuest and Sinn (2015, 2016) and Hellwig (2015a, b, c), who initially had expressed a different opinion. The special internal calculation methods for achieving this result differ between the ELA, ANFA and PSPP assets, but the end result is always the one described in the text, as was confirmed by the Bundesbank in a letter to Fuest and Sinn dated 13 January 2016. See See Fuest and Sinn (2018a, b).

[17] Explicitly including the case where the Council decides for the mutualization of risks would make the subsequent equations more complicated, because in some cases the actual rates of returns of monetary assets rather than the main refinancing rate would have to be considered. However, if the mathematical expectation of the actual rates of return that are subject to pooling is equal to the main refinancing rate, as a capital market equilibrium with risk neutral investors would imply, equation (9.2), as well as the final equation for the effective rate of interest derived from it, would not change if this effective rate of interest were interpreted in terms of mathematical expectations.

[18] See European Central Bank (2014a).

[19] In addition, there is a separate interest rate on LTROs and the marginal lending facility.

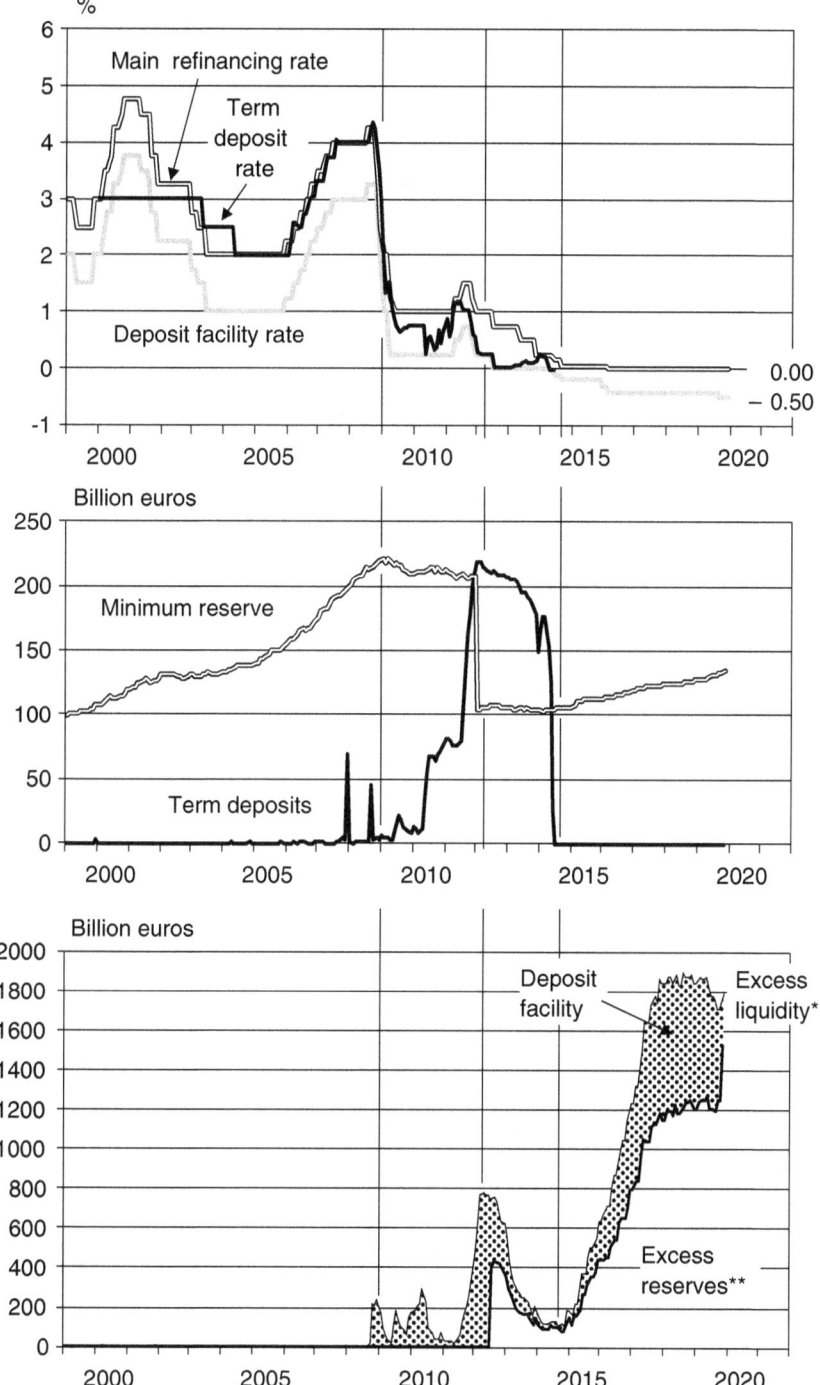

Fig. 9.1 Policy interest rates and deposits in the Eurosystem. *Excess liquidity = excess reserves + deposit facility. **Excess reserves = ordinary demand deposits − minimum reserves. Remark: Minimum reserves were reduced from 2% to 1% of deposits on 18 January 2012. All data refer to end-of-month data. Before summer 2012, when the

Equation (9.7) shows that the liquidity inflow, as measured by the sum of Target and cash balances, $T_i + S_i$, can only be used for a limited number of purposes, and these can all be found on the right-hand side of (9.6). The liquidity inflow can change the stock of base money G_i via the stock of minimum reserves M_i (perhaps because a capital flight from abroad has augmented the volume of private bank deposits) and excess liquidity U_i. And if it does not change the stock of base money, commercial banks must either invest it in time deposits L_i or use it for redemption of money creation credits A_i. As explained in Chap. 7, the latter typically means the repayment of refinancing loans. However, in principle it could also be a repurchase of securities from the NCB, for example when the QE program is reversed.

Equation (9.7) is algebraic and hence specifies both the sources and sinks of international liquidity flows whose accumulated volume is measured by the Target and cash balances. The sources are the origins of the liquidity flown out from the debtor countries, and the sinks the uses of the liquidity in the creditor countries. Both, sources and sinks, are in principle characterized by G_i, L_i, A_i, M_i and U_i with the appropriate signs and subscripts attached. As the inflow in one country is the outflow from others, there is always more than one country involved in influencing country i's redistribution gain Z_i. According to (9.3) this influence is exerted by changing both the primary interest income of NCB i and the primary interest income Y_{i*} that other NCBs earn.

Note that the statutory amount of cash circulating in any country i, $\bar{B}_i$, is assumed to be constant, unable to serve as a potential sink or source of liquidity. In the Eurozone's definition of the cash balance as explained in Chap. 4, any extra cash issued by the local NCB beyond $\bar{B}_i$ is regarded as a physical export of banknotes, given that the true physical flow of banknotes cannot be

---

Fig. 9.1 (continued) deposit facility rate was positive, excess reserves were approximately zero. The deviations from zero were too small to be visible in the diagram. In September 2019, the ECB introduced huge interest-free tiers for excess reserves which subsequently lead to a sharp rise in excess reserves, a topic that will be discussed in Chap. 10. (Source: Sinn (2019a), based on European Central Bank, Statistical Data Warehouse, *Eurosystem Policy and Exchange Rates*, Official interest rates, Key ECB interest rates, http://sdw.ecb.europa.eu/browse.do?node=9691107; Minimum reserves and liquidity, http://sdw.ecb.europa.eu/browse.do?node=9691109; Eurosystem balance sheet, Eurosystem consolidated statement, http://sdw.ecb.europa.eu/browse.do?node=9691294-; Deutsche Bundesbank, *Geldpolitische Geschäfte des Eurosystems (Tenderverfahren)*, https://www.bundesbank.de/resource/blob/607812/56b28363cb29bd223e1cd202f62e4bfb/mL/refd-data.pdf.)

monitored. Thus, when NCB i issues more banknotes, this is counted as a negative impact on its cash balance as is shown by equation (7.2) in Chap. 7.

The next section formally derives an expression for the marginal effective rate of interest on Target and cash balances of a particular NCB. The discussion is limited to marginal effects, because, as with any normal portfolio model, marginal and average rates of return may differ. Note also that while it is true that Target and cash balances measure international liquidity shifts and therefore result in intra-Eurosystem interest flows by way of pooling, pooling may lead to an international redistribution of primary income for other reasons as well. For example, an intra-country shift between an NCB's assets and liabilities as shown on the right-hand side of (9.6) that would change an NCB's primary income would also be partly "taxed" away by the pooling mechanism. With these qualifications, the effective marginal rate of interest can be calculated in Sect. 9.3.

9.5 The Interest Formula

The marginal effective rate of interest on Target and cash balances of a particular NCB i, ρ_i, as defined in equation (9.4) depends on how the international liquidity shift measured by the balances affects the participating NCBs' interest-generating assets and interest-costing deposits. To be able to derive a formal expression it is necessary to specify a set of coefficients that indicate a country's marginal structure of the sinks and sources of the international liquidity flows. To be more specific, assumptions are needed as to what proportions a marginal inflow of liquidity $d(T_i + S_i)$ stems from the sources or fills the sinks specified in equation (9.6). Let γ_i, $0 \le \gamma_i \le 1$, denote the proportion of the incoming liquidity used to increase the local monetary base,

$$dG_i = \gamma_i d(T_i + S_i), \tag{9.8}$$

while the remainder, $1 - \gamma_i$, denotes the proportion flowing into term deposits or being used to repay money creation credit, the respective sub-proportions being λ_i and $1 - \lambda_i$, $0 \le \lambda_i \le 1$:

$$dL_i = \lambda_i(1-\gamma_i)d(T_i + S_i), \quad dA_i = -(1-\lambda_i)(1-\gamma_i)d(T_i + S_i). \tag{9.9}$$

Finally, let μ_i, $0 \le \mu_i \le 1$, be the proportion of the increase in the monetary base that is flowing into minimum reserves, while $1 - \mu_i$ is the proportion accumulated as excess liquidity:

$$dM_i = \mu_i dG_i, \quad dU_i = (1-\mu_i)dG_i. \tag{9.10}$$

Figure 9.2 summarizes these assumptions and assists in remembering how the coefficients are defined. Note that the assumptions made imply that the liquidity inflow as measured by $d(T + S)$ must go somewhere. Thus, when the policy interest rates are positive, there is no possibility for the incremental

Fig. 9.2 The marginal structure of sinks (and sources) of international liquidity flows as measured by the Target and cash balances. (Note: This graph is to be understood algebraically, that is the coefficients would also apply to the case of a liquidity outflow where *M, U, L* and *–A* are sources rather than sinks of liquidity)

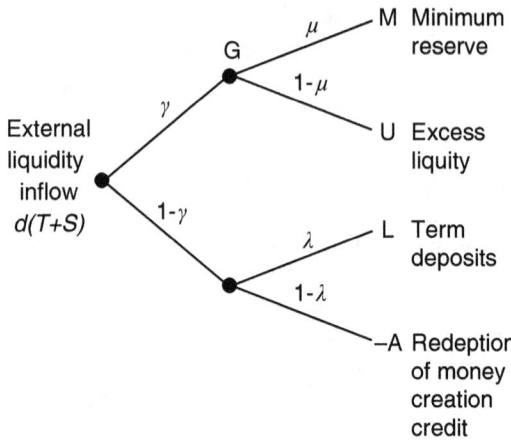

Target and cash balances not to change NCB *i*'s primary seignorage income subject to pooling.

If account is taken of the fact that all Target and cash balances add up to zero in the entire Eurozone, it follows that

$$d(T_{i*} + S_{i*}) = -d(T_i + S_i), \quad (9.11)$$

where *i** again indicates the aggregate of all other NCBs except *i*. Differentiation of (9.4), using the definition of Y_i and, accordingly, Y_{i*}, as given by (9.6), as well as (9.7), (9.8), (9.9) and (9.10), yields

$$\rho_i = \alpha_i \tilde{\rho}_{i*} + (1 - \alpha_i) \tilde{\rho}_i, \quad (9.12)$$

where

$$\tilde{\rho}_j = \gamma_j \left(\mu_j r + (1-\mu_j) r^U \right) + (1-\gamma_j)\left(\lambda_j r^L + (1-\lambda_j) r \right), \quad j = i, i^*, \quad (9.13)$$

and ρ_i is the marginal effective rate of interest on Target and cash balances as defined in (9.5). ρ_i measures the pooling-induced flow of intra-Eurosystem seignorage income that is caused by a marginal increase in country *i*'s Target and cash balances. In (9.13) half of the reaction coefficients refer to liquidity sinks in country *i* and half analogously to liquidity sources in the aggregate of the rest of the Eurozone, labeled *i**. Suppose a unit of liquidity $d(T_i + S_i)$ is transferred from the rest of the Eurozone, *i**, to country *i*. The variable $\tilde{\rho}_{i*}$ is the subsequent marginal *increase* of primary seignorage income of NCBs *i** and $\tilde{\rho}_i$ is the corresponding marginal *reduction* of primary seignorage income of NCB *i*, where both the increase and the reduction are absorbed by the pool. Both determine the marginal effective intra-Eurosystem interest rate on the

Target and cash balances according to (9.4) and (9.6), where subscript i is replaced with i^*, if appropriate, as is summarized in equation (9.12).

The complexity of this expression can be reduced in two prominent and relevant cases, because they render the distinction between $\tilde{\rho}_{i^*}$ and $\tilde{\rho}_i$ irrelevant:

(a) *The small-country case*: Here $\alpha_i \approx 0$. Country i's influence on the aggregate pooling volume and its refund is negligible, and what counts for its redistribution gain is only the reduction in its own primary seignorage, which reduces the delivery to the pool. Pooling now compensates nearly exactly for the reduction of primary seignorage, which results from the liquidity inflow measured by the increase in the Target and cash balance. So all terms with subscript i^* drop out of the equations. Perhaps Luxembourg or Malta qualify as examples for this case.

(b) *Symmetry case*: Country i is an "average" type in the sense that the structure of its marginal liquidity sources or sinks is the same as the respective structure of the aggregate of the other countries ($\tilde{\rho}_i = \tilde{\rho}_{i^*}$).

In both cases, equations (9.12) and (9.13) imply the following simplified equation for the effective marginal rate of interest on the Target and cash balances:

$$\rho = \gamma\left(\mu r + (1-\mu)r^U\right) + (1-\gamma)\left(\lambda r^L + (1-\lambda)r\right) \text{ for } \alpha_i \approx 0 \text{ and / or } \tilde{\rho} = \tilde{\rho}_{i^*}, \quad (9.14)$$

where the subscript i was dropped because it is no longer needed.[20]

To interpret this equation let us concentrate on the more important symmetry case b), which covers small and large countries alike. Assume first that there is no possibility for the banks to hold time deposits with the NCB and that the inflowing liquidity is used by the banks to reduce interest-bearing money creation credit ($\lambda = \gamma = 0$), which keeps the monetary base in country i constant. Then (9.14) reduces to $\rho = r$, such that the Target and cash balances bear the main refinancing rate. This is a special case that has already been dealt with by Fuest and Sinn (2015, 2016, 2018a, b) and Sinn (2018c, p. 32n).[21] It

---

[20] Note that with positive policy interest rates, even though more Target and cash balances by necessity imply more redistribution among the NCBs and hence a positive effective marginal rate of intra-Eurosystem interest on these balances, it does not follow that, conversely, there would be no redistribution without such balances. The simple reason is that all assumptions made refer only to marginal reaction coefficients. For example, an NCB in whose territory commercial banks borrow more than average excess liquidity from it, say because of peculiarities of national banking regulation, would have to share the extra interest revenue it collects with the rest of the Eurozone even in cases where its balances are zero. Nevertheless, increasing this NCB's Target liability would, under the above assumptions, imply even larger redistribution losses.

[21] Basically, the argument was already raised against De Grauwe and Ji (2012); see Sinn (2012d) for a rejoinder.

corresponds to the analysis in Chaps. 5 and 6 and assumes that the reallocation of refinancing loans between the countries fully compensates for the liquidity outflows and inflows as measured by the Target and cash balances.[22] The refinancing loans of the NCB of a country in crisis now replace the dwindling private foreign credit, if not outright capital flight; negative Target and/or cash balances arise there, and the NCB in the first instance benefits from the extra interest on the additional refinancing loans issued. However, this additional interest income is made available to other NCBs with positive balances by means of interest pooling and compensates for the loss of interest due to the displacement of domestic refinancing loans. The displacement takes place because the banks of the creditor countries do not need the incoming liquidity and thus redeem the refinancing credit they had taken before. The interest income of the single NCBs does not change despite the rising Target and cash balances, because the interest flow through the pooling mechanism compensates the creditor NCB that loses primary interest income and burdens the debtor NCB that gains primary interest income.

However, the Target and cash balances do not have to go hand in hand with a relocation of money creation credits. If instead they came about solely due to a shift in term deposits, the constellation $\rho = r^L$ for $\lambda = 1$, $\gamma = 0$ would prevail. Now, the relevant interest rate for the balances would be the term deposit rate. This case is currently not relevant though because the term deposits have been suspended since mid-2014.

What is more important is the special case in which the Target and cash balances arise from the relocation of deposits that commercial banks hold with their NCBs while the money creation credits of the participating countries stay unchanged. In this case, the liquidity flows change the minimum reserves or the excess liquidity that banks hold with their NCBs.

If the minimum reserves absorb the entire liquidity shift, we have $\rho = r$ for $\gamma = \mu = 1$. While it is hard to imagine that this case could ever prevail, given that only a fraction of a private deposit flight of bank customers would affect the minimum deposits while the entire deposit flight would show up in Target balances, a combination with a reallocation of money creation credit as described above is not implausible. The effective marginal rate of interest in this case would obviously be the refinancing rate r. This gives the refinancing rate a prominent role in determining the effective rate of interest on Target balances.

Finally, consider the case where the liquidity flows measured by increasing Target and cash balances only involve compensating changes in the stocks of excess liquidity. Now, equation (9.14) reduces to the constellation $\rho = r^U$ for $\gamma = 1$, $\mu = 0$; i.e. the deposit facility rate now is the relevant measure for the effective marginal rate of interest on the Target and cash balances.

---

[22] See Sinn and Wollmershäuser (2011, 2012), European Central Bank (2011, footnote p. 37), Sinn (2012a, 2014a, 2015b).

9.6 The Currently Negative Rate of Interest on Target and Cash Balances

As Fig. 9.1 revealed, the deposit facility rate has been negative since 2014. This has obvious implications for the effective rate of interest on Target and cash balances. As the main refinancing rate r has been practically zero[23] since 2015, while term deposits were no longer allowed, Equation (9.14) implies that for an Eurozone economy with an average marginal liquidity structure, the effective marginal rate of interest on Target and cash balances is currently given by

$$\rho = \gamma(1-\mu)r^U < 0 \text{ for } r = 0,\ \lambda = 0,\ \gamma > 0,\ \mu < 1. \qquad (9.15)$$

This expression shows that when the interest rate for money creation credit is zero and term deposits are not allowed ($\lambda = 0$), the effective marginal rate of interest on Target and cash balances is equal to the deposit facility rate r^U times the proportion of the international liquidity shift that involves changes in excess liquidity $\gamma(1 - \mu)$ rather than changes in the minimum reserve or the stock of money creation credit. It follows that a negative deposit rate translates into a negative effective marginal rate of Target and cash balances provided that only some of the international liquidity flow measured by a change of these balances involves the banks' excess reserves.

Given that, at this writing, the deposit facility rate is 0.5 percent, the effective marginal rate of interest on Target and cash balances would be 0.25% if half of the sources and sinks were excess liquidity and the other half minimum reserves or money creation credit.

9.7 Compound Interest and the Transfer of Liquidity and Income

If the pooling mechanism implies that the liquidity flows measured by increasing Target and cash balances involve subsequent intra-Eurosystem interest flows, the question arises as to what these interest payments actually mean. As was explained above, they are recorded as additional Target claims and liabilities, but they are more than just internal accounting items within the Eurosystem. In addition, they do involve income and liquidity transfers between the non-central bank sectors of the economies involved, because these sectors deliver more interest to the local NCB in one country and less interest in the other. This was explained in detail in Sect. 9.3 and is the essence of equations (9.12) and (9.13)

Note, however, that this does not yet involve real international resource transfers. Other things being equal, the intra-Eurosystem interest flows in principle, that is with positive policy interest rates, are instead simply booked as additional

---

[23] The main refinancing rate has been equal to 0.05% in 2015 and turned zero in 2016, where it has been up to this writing. See Fig. 9.1.

Target balances, that is as additional claims in the balance sheets of the creditor NCBs and additional liabilities in those of the debtor NCBs.[24] This is very similar to private international interest flows carried out by way of payment orders within the Eurozone which also involve booking more Target claims and liabilities.

A real resource transfer that would avoid booking higher Target balances upon paying the interest is only possible by countervailing transactions of the non-central bank sectors. For example, the economic agents of the Target and cash balance debtor country could sell an appropriate amount of real estate, stocks, securities or gold, or they could borrow in the private interbank market, thus giving foreign banks a credit title at market conditions. Alternatively, they could export more goods and services or reduce their imports. All these measures would lead to net payment orders from the creditor countries to the debtor countries and, if they have the right size, would compensate for the booking of the interest flows in the Target accounts.

Let us consider another possibility though. Suppose there is no debt service in terms of countervailing real transactions and in fact no other international payment orders or physical cash transports that would also affect the balances. An interesting question is whether the booking of intra-Eurosystem interest payments in the Target accounts would in this case imply compound interest in a similar way as private unsettled credit accounts would do.

This question is not trivial, as inside the universe of the Eurosystem payments are not simply made with euros, given that all NCBs can make them themselves anyway. The compound interest question is important, because if credit relationships grow at a compound rate, credit debtors would progressively lose their wealth and might head towards bankruptcy. Although the risk of bankruptcy will not be discussed in more depth until Chap. 12, it is useful to prepare that discussion here.

To be specific, let us ask: Can an intra-Eurosystem interest flow resulting from the pooling process that takes place in year 1 and is booked in the Target balances lead to a secondary increase in Target balances in year 2, a tertiary increase in year 3 and so on? The answer cannot be found in the bylaws of the Eurosystem which, indeed, speak nowhere of compound interest.

The answer instead lies in the fact that the reallocation of seignorage by way of intra-Eurosystem interest flows, which is caused by the pooling process, involves an extraction of liquidity from the economies of the debtor NCBs and injection of liquidity into the economies of the creditor NCBs that changes the monetary aggregates once again and again triggers more intra-Eurosystem interest flows.

Suppose that the initial payment orders that built up Target and cash balances occurred in year 0 and that the subsequent intra-Eurosystem interest flows take place in year 1.

These intra-Eurosystem interest flows have two effects. Firstly, as mentioned, they are booked as additional claims and liabilities, respectively, in the NCB's Target balances from where they enter the overall annual balance sheets.

---

[24] See e.g. the treatment of interest on cash balances: European Central Bank (2001, article 2, paragraph 3; 2016g, article 2, paragraph 3)

Secondly, the liquidity withdrawals from the economies of the debtor NCBs and the injections of liquidity into the economies of the creditor NCBs, which cause these intra-Eurosystem interest flows result in changes in monetary aggregates, as booked in the balance sheets. To be specific, term deposits, excess liquidity and minimum reserves on the liability side of the debtor NCBs' balance sheets shrink and/or money creation credits booked on the asset side rise to the extent of the liquidity withdrawal caused by the intra-Eurosystem interest flows. These entries just outweigh the additional Target liabilities in the debtor NCBs' balances sheets in year 1 that also result from these intra-Eurosystem interest flows.[25] And of course the reverse is true in the creditor countries.

In year 2, the new interest-induced changes in the monetary aggregates as booked in the balance sheets of year 1 of necessity again increase the primary interest income extracted from the economies of the debtor NCBs and vice versa with the creditor NCBs. These secondary changes in primary interest income will again be outweighed by additional Target liabilities with the debtor NCBs and by additional Target claims with the creditors NCBs in year 2.

Additional intra-Eurosystem interest payments from the debtor NCBs to the creditor NCBs will have to be booked in the Target balances in year 3, and they are again outweighed by the changes in monetary aggregates, and so on.

Year by year, the base for collecting primary interest income shrinks with the creditor NCBs and grows with the debtor NCBs so that more and more intra-Eurosystem income and liquidity transfers are necessary that are booked in the Target balances and ensure that the secondary distribution of interest income among the NCBs stays unchanged. As with any private debtor contract, the compound interest effect leads to growing imbalances over time, provided of course that the policy interest rates are positive.[26]

To formalize this finding, consider the situation from the viewpoint of a single creditor NCB i, facing a group of other NCBs i^* that attain a debtor position. Let $d(T_i(0) + S_i(0))$ be an exogenously caused additional liquidity inflow with a corresponding Target and cash balance claim, which is booked in the balance sheet by the end of year 0. The inflow of liquidity changes the monetary aggregates and reduces NCB i's primary interest revenue in year 1.

---

[25] A colleague has doubted that there is compound interest on Target balances pointing to a special clause in the bylaws of the European Central Bank (2016g, article 3, paragraph 2, point 2) according to which a mismatch between earmarkable assets and liabilities shall be offset by applying the main refinancing rate to the difference and forcing the NCB to contribute, or entitling it to collect, this from other NCBs in the pooling process. In the case at hand, there is no mismatch though, as the debtor and creditor NCBs must book the intra-Eurosystem income transfers in their Target balances. Thus, for example, with the creditor NCB, the additional Target claims from booking the redistribution gains are precisely equal to the additional entries on the liability side of its balance sheet resulting from the fact that less liquidity is extracted from the local economy. And of course, the situation in the country with the debtor NCB is the mirror image of this.

[26] This was first mentioned, but not proved, by Sinn (2012a, p. 179). A similar statement has been made by the German Council of Economic Advisors (Sachverständigenrat 2018, p. 254), again without giving an explanation.

Pooling compensates for this loss of primary interest revenue by causing intra-Eurosystem interest transfers to NCB i and a corresponding income and liquidity shift to country i in the same year. Likewise, pooling takes away from the other NCBs the extra primary interest income they earn in year 1 because of the original liquidity outflow in year 0. As the intra-Eurosystem interest flow is booked in the Target balances, NCB i's Target balance in year 1 will increase by the relevant effective interest rate of that year, $\rho(1)$, such that $d(T_i(1) + S_i(1)) = d(T_i(0) + S_i(0))(1 + \rho(1))$, and so will the liquidity injected into country i. In principle, $\rho(1)$ is determined by the structure of sources and sinks of liquidity as specified in equation (9.14). The shifting of liquidity due to the intra-Eurosystem interest payments caused by pooling will now again force the foreign NCBs i^* to issue more money creation credit or reduce the various kinds of deposits, while the opposite is true in country i.

In year 2, these changes in monetary aggregates that took place in year 1 again increase the aggregate primary seignorage income of NCBs i^* and reduce that of NCB i, and again pooling will ensure sufficient intra-Eurosystem interest flows to compensate for the differences. Again, the additional interest is booked on the Target accounts in year 2 implying that $d(T_i(2) + S_i(2)) = d(T_i(0) + S_i(0))(1 + \rho(1))(1 + \rho(2))$, while the monetary aggregates change, because of the liquidity extraction and injection involved.

In a similar way, the original, exogenous increase in the Target and cash balances obviously transmits to the consecutive years with a volume that grows at the respective effective rate of interest on the Target and cash balances. By the end of year t, $t > 0$, the sum of the balances is

$$d(T_i(t) + S_i(t)) = (dT_i(0) + dS_i(0))\prod_{k=1}^{t}(1 + \rho(k)), \qquad (9.16)$$

while the same amount of liquidity has been extracted from the economies of NCBs i* and injected into the economy of NCB i, as is reported in the respective entries of monetary aggregates in the balance sheets.

This expression shows that Target debt cannot forever be serviced by merely adding interest and even compound interest to the Target balances because the balances would permanently grow at a rate equal to the effective rate of interest. This would be a problem for the creditor and the debtor countries alike. The creditor countries would be downed in liquidity being eventually forced to absorb it by driving its money creation credit to negative territory, i.e. by borrowing funds from the banking sector. This would be a situation even more extreme than the one in which Germany was in 2012 and 2013, if for other reasons (cf. Fig. 7.1), when its internal base money had fully disappeared. In would eventually involve negative base money. The debtor NCBs in turn would be endangered, because they would risk drying out, while their wealth—the difference between their net assets from other sources and their Target debt—would shrink at a progressive rate and eventually become negative.

Thus, in a sense, booking the intra-Eurosystem interest on Target and cash balances in the Target balances is only a method of writing down the invoice and drives the ECB into more and more asymmetric monetary policies and the economies involved into more and more unsustainable if not dangerous situations. To avoid the potential terrors, genuine international payments of other sectors of the economies are necessary such as payments by firms, commercial banks, private households and governments.

Again, everything is similar to normal credits between private agents. If there is no redemption, interest will just be booked and added to the debt, and the debt grows at the rate of interest. If at least the interest is paid, the credit volume stays constant. And only if the debt service involves both interest and debt redemption, will the credit volume fall.

A final remark is appropriate concerning the currently negative deposit facility rate. As was shown with equation (9.15), this rate also makes the effective rate of interest on Target and cash balances negative provided at least some of the change in Target balances comes along with mere deposit shifts. Thus, currently, the compound interest effect implies that the Target balances decline year by year unless new payment orders between the sectors outside the central banks create new ones. This effect contributed to some extent to the slowdown and ultimate reversal of the Target curves towards the end of the third phase of the crisis according to the categorization of Fig. 5.1. This should not be taken to mean that it was the dominant effect, however. In addition to the temporary halt in QE during the year 2019, there was a further and very strong effect that has been causing a halt if not turnaround of the Target balances in the most recent months shortly before these lines were written. The next chapter will briefly look into this.

CHAPTER 10

Interest Spreads and Tiering

Arguably, the rise of the Target balances largely results from the ECB's resistance to allow growing interest spreads between the countries of the Eurozone, which would have lured in private capital and reduced the liquidity outflows. As the ECB saw international interest spreads as distortions in the transmission of monetary policy, it compensated for liquidity outflows by allowing the respective NCBs to issue and lend out more money. However, out of concern for the concentration of liquidity in only a few countries, above all Germany, the ECB Council ultimately decided to differentiate its marginal policy interest rates. It did so by exempting huge brackets or "tiers" of banks deposits from penalty interest, thus effectively differentiating the marginal deposit rates between the countries. The differentiation immediately implied bank lending from liquidity abundant countries like Germany to the liquidity scarce Mediterranean countries in order to exploit the unexploited bracket space, which reduced the Target balances.

10.1   The Interest-induced Shift of Liquidity, Interest Spreads and the Elasticity of Local Money Supply

The last chapter has shown that the international liquidity shift measured by the Target and cash balances by necessity induces a subsequent intra-Eurosystem interest flow from the debtor to the creditor countries by way of pooling the seignorage income.[1] Pooling compensates for the fact that the former collect more, and the latter less, primary interest income from the non-central bank

---

[1] Recall that these statements refer to marginal effects. As explained, intra-Eurosystem redistributive flows not only result from international liquidity shifts as measured by the Target and cash balances, but may also result from intra-country liquidity shifts between the NCBs' assets and liabilities. The subsequent discussion abstracts from these shifts and assumes for simplicity that there would not be intra-Eurosystem interest redistribution without Target and cash balances. This is not essential for the discussion.

sectors, provided of course that the policy interest rates are positive (as they aren't at this writing).

As we have seen, the intra-Eurosystem extraction of more interest from countries whose NCBs build up Target and cash debtor positions and less interest from the respective creditor countries shifts income and liquidity across the borders in a similar way as normal international interest flows between private agents would do. As there is compound interest, the original liquidity transfer measured by the initial Target and cash liability grows at the effective intra-Eurosystem rate of interest on the Target balances. Other things being equal, the permanent extraction of liquidity (Target and cash balance) from the debtor countries would eventually dry up the economies of these countries and make the creditor economies more and more liquid.

This would, however, prompt obvious reactions of the capital market. The liquidity extraction would raise the local market interest rates in the debtor economies as banks and private agents would try to borrow from abroad and offer the lenders better rates, while the opposite would be true in the creditor economies, as more and more liquidity piles up there.

The strength of this effect depends on the elasticity with which the Eurosystem reacts to the international liquidity transfers, that is how much it is willing to compensate for the scarcer or more abundant liquidity, respectively, by inducing or tolerating compensating changes the stocks of local money creation credit. Unless the system reacts perfectly elastically, interest spreads between the countries will grow over time.

These spreads have two effects. For one, they induce private capital flows from the creditor countries to the debtor countries. These capital flows reduce the Target and cash balances, as they involve payment orders by the creditor countries. The capital flows can be seen as a kind of debt rescheduling action for the NCBs, because the intra-Eurosystem interest flows and perhaps even the Target and cash balance credits are replaced with private capital.

For another, the interest spreads reduce private investment in the debtor countries and increase it in the creditor countries, with the result that the economies weaken in the former and pick up in the latter. The weakening economies will import less and the strengthening economies will import more. The changes in imports will result in net payment orders from the creditor to the debtor countries and thus also reduce the balances.

Interest rate differentials within a currency union were common before World War II in the US, which, with its twelve district central banks, bears some similarities to the Eurosystem. Money was scarce, and asymmetrical lending by local central banks triggered ISA balances. As explained in Chap. 2, ISA balances were similar to the Target balances, except that the debtor central banks had to settle their ISA debt with gold. The gold settlement reduced the incentive of local central banks of compensating for liquidity outflows with newly created credit money and made their money supply inelastic. So, considerable spreads of the Federal Funds Rate emerged at the time, often 100 basis points and more.[2]

Yet the ECB did not like interest rate differentials, spoke of a disturbance in the process of transmitting its monetary policy, and tried to compensate for the missing liquidity with the sophisticated policy measures described above in Chaps. 5, 6 and 8 (collateral policy, ELA, ANFA, SMP, OMT, QE etc.). The measures had in common that they all avoided the liquidity squeeze in the Target and cash balance debtor countries. Some reduced the Target balances because they induced or were counted as private capital flows (SMP and OMT), and others (ELA, ANFA, QE) increased them even more, because they induced public capital flows through the Eurosystem.

The ECB also effectively eliminated the ongoing leakage of liquidity which resulted from the compound interest effect by reducing the policy interest rates to zero and by even pushing them into negative territory. Thereby, it reversed the interest-driven liquidity flow, allowing the debtor countries to order more goods and assets from abroad without increasing their Target debt.

However, in fear of violating the boundaries of its mandate, the ECB again and again pressed policy makers to take over by organizing fiscal rescue systems if not outright transfers (fiscal union), which would induce countervailing payment orders and hence reduce the balances. The parliaments of the euro member states, however, feared their electorates and were very reluctant to follow suit.[3]

Thus, in the end, the ball was back in the court of the ECB which realized that its ammunition had been used up. It ultimately gave in and accepted that spreads in its policy rates would be necessary to reduce the Target balances.

10.2 Differentiating the Interest Rates by Way of Tiering

For the first time in its history, the ECB in September 2019 decided to differentiate its policy interest rates between the countries of the Eurozone.[4] In the Target creditor countries where liquidity had piled up, the marginal deposit facility rate was implicitly set 0.5 percentage points lower for most banks than in the Target debtor countries where the liquidity injected through the QE program did not stick, as was explained in Chap. 8.

The trick by which this was done is *tiering*. Banks were given an interest-free bracket or "tier" for their excess reserves equal to six times the minimum reserve. By the end of 2019, the volume of this bracket was €805 billion while the excess liquidity was €1786 billion, as was shown in Fig. 9.1. Thus the interest-free brackets were nearly half of the excess liquidity (45%). This is a truly huge volume.

---

[2] See Chandler (1958) and European Economic Advisory Group (2013, Figure 4.3, p. 103).
[3] See the chronology ("The six steps of the crisis") in Sinn (2014a, pp. 257–69).
[4] European Central Bank (2019c).

This immediately meant that all banks tried to shift as much money as they could from their deposit facilities into their excess reserves to fill the interest free bracket space that the ECB Council had suddenly opened up. This shift is clearly visible on the right-hand side of the lowest graph of the triple Fig. 9.1 in Chap. 9.

More importantly, however, it also meant that those banks that could not fill their brackets by shifting funds from the deposit facility, because they did not have enough liquidity, contracted with others that had surplus liquidity not only beyond the minimum reserves but beyond the new interest-free brackets. As the second group of banks would have had to pay a penalty interest rate of 0.5% on their marginal excess reserves while the first group could park these reserves interest-free, both parties were able to profit from this contract if they agreed on credits with an intermediate interest rate r^b, $0 > r^b > -0.5\%$.

As the banks with surplus liquidity almost by definition would be sitting in the Target creditor countries, the immediate implication of these contracts was a reduction in the Target balances.[5] Small wonder that banks made use of this to a very large extent and that the Target balances of the liquidity-abundant and liquidity-poor countries both shrank in absolute terms. This is the explanation for the rapid decline in the Target balances as shown in the most recent data in Fig. 5.1.

How far will the decline in Target balances go? Theoretically, if all brackets could be filled with surplus reserves above the brackets and all surplus reserves were located in Target creditor countries, while the entire free bracket space were located in Target debtor countries, the Target debt could decline by €805 billion. But of course it is implausible that this assumption is true, as there will probably be not only mismatches of liquidity across but also within the countries. Moreover, the maximum risk premium the creditors could earn would be 0.5%, or 50 basis points. That may be too little to convince many investors to put substantial parts of their surplus reserves at risk in deposits of countries from where they had fled in the first place.

The ECB downplayed its tiering decision in its communications, but given that it induced such a rapid change in the Target balances and is a fundamental deviation from the dogma that short-term policy interest rates should be the same everywhere in the Eurozone, it is justified to associate the new decision with a new phase in the development and management of the Eurozone crisis, as is done in Fig. 5.1.

Interestingly enough, as with the QE decision, the Target balances had already moved some months before the actual decision was made in the direction which had become plausible to many observers only in retrospect, including myself. This can be attributed in all likelihood to the cleverness of investment bankers, some of whom were particularly good forecasters of what would happen, to put it politely. Before the asset purchases under QE were formally decided, many investors bought them already at favorable conditions in the

---

[5] See Sinn (2019c).

market, because they knew that they soon would be able to resell them with a profit to their local NCBs. This reduced the Target balances of the Mediterranean countries even before the formal QE decision in January 2015 of the ECB Council, because their government bonds were once distributed over the world given that they had previously financed their current account deficits with them. And before tiering was decided in September 2019, the banks of the Mediterranean countries that had large unexploited brackets borrowed in the interbank market at more favorable conditions than were later available when everyone would know what had been decided. The reader may wish to study Fig. 5.1 in detail to find out which of all countries had bankers with the very best forecasting abilities.

10.3 The Effective Marginal Rate of Interest with Non-uniform Policy Rates

A final word may be useful concerning the implications of having different policy interest rates for the effective marginal rate of interest on Target and cash balances. While equations (9.6) and (9.12) to (9.16) in Chap. 9 all assumed uniform policy rates, these equations can easily be generalized to the case of non-uniform rates. Assume there are just two different kinds of policy rates of each type, one for countries i^* and one for countries or country i and characterize the policy rates in equation (9.6) by these two different subscripts, respectively. Then it is straightforward that instead of (9.12) and (9.13) we get

$$\rho_i = \alpha_i \tilde{\rho}_{i^*} + (1-\alpha_i) \tilde{\rho}_i, \tag{10.1}$$

and

$$\tilde{\rho}_j = \gamma_j \left(\mu_j r_j + (1-\mu_j) r_j^U \right) + (1-\gamma_j) \left(\lambda_j r_j^L + (1-\lambda_j) r_j \right), \ j = i, i^*. \tag{10.2}$$

As of this writing, as was explained in Box 9.2 in Chap. 9, term deposits are no longer allowed ($\lambda_i = \lambda_{i^*} = 0$), and the main refinancing rate is zero ($r_i = r_{i^*} = 0$). In this case, (10.1) and (10.2) imply

$$\rho_i = \alpha_i \gamma_{i^*} (1-\mu_{i^*}) r_{i^*}^U + (1-\alpha_i) \gamma_i (1-\mu_i) r_i^U$$
$$\text{for } r_i, r_{i^*} = 0, \ \lambda_i, \lambda_{i^*} = 0, \ \gamma_i, \gamma_{i^*} > 0, \ \mu_i, \mu_{i^*} < 1. \tag{10.3}$$

To analyze the effect of the most recent tiering decision, assume in addition that the unused brackets have not been fully exhausted.[6] Let i^* denote the

---

[6] If they are fully exhausted, the equations of Chap. 9 all stay valid.

countries with unused bracket space ($r_{i*}^U = 0$) and i those with surplus liquidity. Now (10.3) simplifies to

$$\rho_i = (1-\alpha_i)\gamma_i(1-\mu_i)r_i^U < 0 \quad \text{for} \quad r_i^U < 0,\ 0 < \alpha_i < 1,\ \gamma_i > 0,\ \mu_i < 1, \quad (10.4)$$

provided at least some of the liquidity outflow induced by the tiering decision and measured by the decline in country i's Target balance comes from excess liquidity deposits. The equation shows that the effective marginal rate of interest is still negative but less strongly than equation (9.15) revealed, since the first term in brackets on the right-hand side, $(1 - \alpha_i)$ is smaller than one. The explanation is that a reduction in the Target balances of country i which implies less penalty interest in i is not countered by the increase in penalty interest in country i^* as would have been the case before the tiering decision. Thus, tiering implies less redistribution and hence a lower absolute value of the marginal effective rate of intra-Eurosystem interest on Target and cash balances. Note that the difference between (9.15) and (10.3) would disappear in the small-country case where $\alpha_i \approx 0$.

10.4 A Lesson to be Learned

Given the strong and obvious incentive effect of differentiated policy interest rates on the Target balances, one may wonder why the ECB had not resorted to this policy tool before. The answer may lie in the disparate experiences many countries of the Eurozone had made in the pre-euro period when they persistently had to cope with the mistrust of markets in their creditworthiness which forced their firms and public institutions to pay very high interest rates, straining their budgets. This is why the ECB's Governing Council developed the view that similar market interest rates with rather low spreads are a sign of a functioning currency union. Equal policy interest rates would contribute to reducing the spreads at which markets are trading.

After all, with some qualifications, the attempt to reduce the enormous interest rate differentials in the years before the euro seems to have been a major incentive for many countries to join the common currency in the first place. The expectation to be able to borrow in a currency that one could not only print at home, but that other countries would accept as legal tender, was rightly translated into the hope that the interest spreads would disappear or at least shrink strongly. That this expectation was indeed fulfilled is shown in Fig. 10.1.

When the euro was ultimately and firmly decided at the Madrid Summit 1995, the interest spreads between Italy, Spain and Portugal on the one hand and Germany on the other were in the order of 500 basis points. But thereafter they disappeared very quickly until May 1998, because that was the point in time when the exchange rates were to be irrevocably fixed. Even the Greek

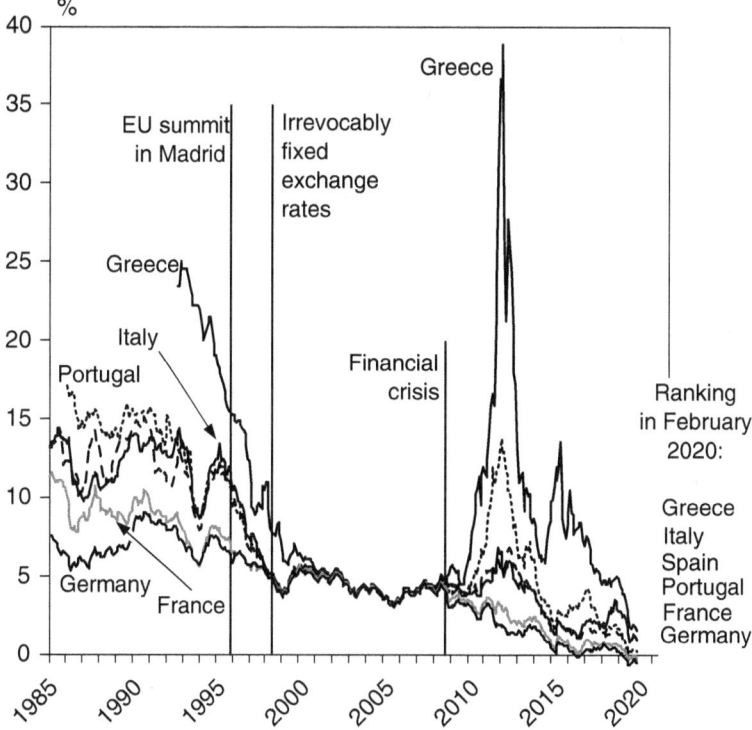

Fig. 10.1 Interest rates for ten-year government bonds among today's Eurozone countries. (Note: The interest rates correspond to average yields for government bonds with ten-year maturity (so-called Benchmark Bonds). Reuters calculates the yield of a fictitious ten-year bond issued on a given date, applying the theory of expectations for interest rates to the observed yields of various instruments with different maturities at that particular date. Source: Thomson Reuters Datastream, interest Rates, benchmark bonds)

interest rate, which had been about 25%, converged very quickly once it was clear that the country would be able to join the euro, if with a delay. This favorable situation lasted only until the outbreak of the financial crisis that culminated in 2008. Thereafter, the spreads grew even more than before and peaked in the crisis of 2012. They again decreased in the sequel, because the OMT program ("whatever it takes"), which basically was a public credit default insurance, had largely eliminated the investment risk. However, up to this writing the spreads never returned to the low levels that temporarily had prevailed in the first few years of the euro, indicating that despite the voluminous protection measures taken by the Eurosystem and the EU, investors still do not believe that all government bonds belong to the same risk class.

Given this history, it is understandable that the view that interest rates should not be differentiated among the Eurozone countries is widespread.

It is wrong nevertheless, as functioning capital markets do need significant interest spreads as signals that contain excessive borrowing. When the likelihood that a debt becomes unsustainable increases, creditors demand higher interest rates, and at higher interest rates debtors lose their appetite in borrowing even more.

In fact, higher notional interest rates are necessary to ensure that the mathematically expected rate of interest is the same for all assets of equal maturity. Suppose q_i is the notional annual rate of interest of an asset i and π_i is the annual probability of default. Then the mathematically expected rate of interest is $q_i - \pi_i$. The most fundamental law in economics is the Law of one Price. Applied to rates of return on any two different kinds of assets i and j of equal maturity but different default risks it requires that $q_i - \pi_i = q_j - \pi_j$. This obviously implies that $q_i > q_j$ for $\pi_i > \pi_j$, i.e. that the asset with the higher default probability does need a higher rate of interest.

With its policy of reducing the interest spreads below what the Law of one Price would have required, the ECB has helped those firms and institutions that had a higher default probability or the country to which they belonged had a higher exit probability than it found justified by market fundamentals. By fixing equal policy rates for banks, it undercut market spreads and made it possible for banks to enjoy arbitrage gains by borrowing from their NCBs rather than in the interbank market. With a grain of salt this can be seen as the major explanation for the emergence of Target balances in the first phase of the Euro crisis and their subsequent reduction after the OMT decision of the Governing Council, which started Phase II, as was explained in Chaps. 5 and 6. The reader may wish to compare Figs. 5.1 and 10.1. The strong correlation between the turn-arounds in Target balances and interest spreads is striking and immediately obvious without resorting to econometric techniques.

Under normal conditions, the Law of one Price has important allocative benefits as it ensures that the world's stock of capital is invested in a way that maximizes aggregate output and welfare. Seen from that perspective, the ECB made a mistake by not respecting the market spreads, providing in fact an implicit interest subsidy to those countries that were distrusted by markets. The ECB countered this view by arguing that at the time preceding the peak of the euro crisis in 2012 and its OMT decision markets were overly pessimistic, requiring much higher interest rates from some countries than was justified by the fundamentals. Markets were wrong when they assessed a non-zero probability to the break-up of the Eurozone.[7] The European Court of Justice adopted and supported this view in its OMT ruling, arguing that there were in fact no systemic risks that would justify the spreads.[8] However, given that the OMT program was decided only a few months after Berlusconi and Papandreou, the presidents of Greece and Italy, had negotiated secretly about potential euro

---

[7] Unpublished statement of European Central Bank (2014b, para 66) for the European Court of Justice.

[8] European Court of Justice (2015, paras 76 and 77).

exits of their countries,[9] this position represents political preferences rather than a description of the actual default and exit probabilities.

Whatever the truth, after the initial confidence crisis that disappeared after the OMT decision, (see Fig. 5.1), according to the ECB's own judgment capital markets were free of stress and systemic risks.[10] If the excess liquidity of the Eurosystem that was caused by the massive asset purchases under the QE program nevertheless assembled in Germany and a few other non-Mediterranean countries rather than spreading equally over the Eurozone, the reason can only have been that capital markets did see justified differences in idiosyncratic default risks that the ECB's Governing Council did not want to respect when setting its policy rates.[11]

And indeed there is ample evidence that the creditworthiness of European banks differed enormously in that period. The clearest one is given by the statistics about non-performing loans, as is shown in Fig. 10.2. Thus, for example, even by the end of 2018, Greek banks had 46% non-performing loans in the total loan portfolio, Cyprian banks 39%, and Italy 10%. These are extremely high numbers by all standards that without the implicit and explicit protection of the ECB would long have led to massive waves of bankruptcies.

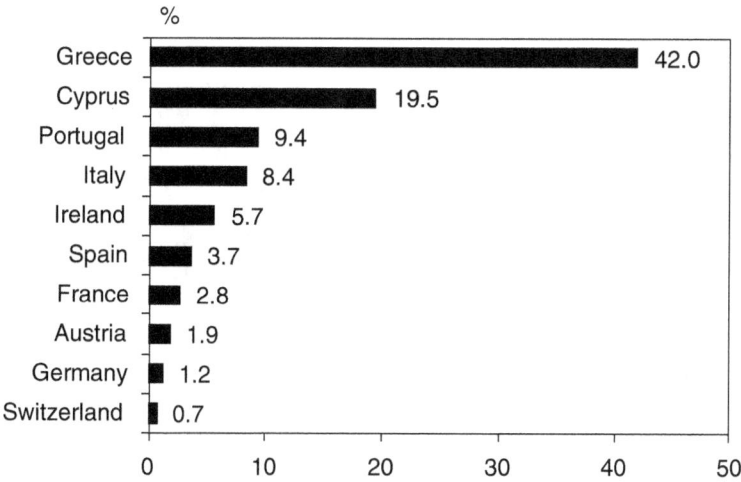

Fig. 10.2 Percentage of non-performing loans in the total loan-portfolio of commercial banks (2018). (Source: IMF, eLibrary-Data, financial soundness indicator, GFSR FSI Tables, Bank non-performing loans to total loans)

---

[9] See Bini Smaghi (2013, Chapter 3: "No turning back", p. 29) and Djankov (2014, p. 3, 17, 105).

[10] See European Central Bank (2016e, p. 22f.).

[11] This is in line with the view of Westermann (2016a, b), according to which the rising Target balances in the QE phase resulted from a preference for safety rather than from technical aspects of the ECB's Asset Purchasing Programme.

In view of this information about non-performing loans, the policy of choosing identical policy interest rates for different national financial systems is problematic. This policy means that the refinancing loans of the Eurosystem are available at much more favorable conditions than similar loans would have been provided by markets. Moreover, banks of the safer countries prefer to hold their liquidity in NCB deposits rather than lending them to banks with a shaky creditworthiness that hardly can offer more interest than they get from similar deposits at home. All of this implies that the excess liquidity of the Eurosystem assembles in only a few countries. The fact that the ECB Governing Council has ultimately given in and has begun to differentiate its policy rates, if only under the cover of "tiering", gives hope that the ECB is gradually moving to a more realistic assessment of the problem of risk spreads.

Interestingly enough, the new ECB President Christine Lagarde (2020a), in her first press conference on Thursday, 12 March 2020, explaining the decisions of the ECB Governing Council, strongly supported this new approach, by stating,

> Well, we will be there, as I said earlier on, using full flexibility, but we are not here to close spreads. This is not the function or the mission of the ECB. There are other tools for that, and there are other actors to actually deal with those issues.

However, given that the international implications of the Corona pandemic meanwhile had become visible, markets were not at all content with this statement. They, in fact, reacted furiously as they saw it as a fundamental and dangerous departure from the policy of reducing the spreads pursued by Lagarde's predecessor Draghi, and they found no relief in the fact that the ECB Governing Council had agreed in the meeting on which Lagarde reported to slightly reduce the policy interest rates to negative territory and to start another asset purchasing program of €120 billion for 2020. They were not satisfied either when Lagarde (2020b) qualified her statement on the same day by returning to usual ECB vocabulary and stating that the Coronavirus would "impair the transmission of monetary policy" and that the ECB would "use the flexibly embedded in the asset purchase programme, including within the public sector purchase programme".[12]

After stock markets crashed on Monday, 16 March, the Governing Council agreed to further expand its asset purchases by another €750 billion in terms of the Pandemic Emergency Purchasing Programme (PEPP) in the late evening of Wednesday, 18 March.[13] This volume was considered to be sufficient and markets stabilized.

---

[12] See the footnote that her administration later added to the protocol of her speech, as reported in Lagarde (2020a).
[13] See ECB (2020a).

CHAPTER 11

The Corona Crisis

From March 2020 onwards the effects of tiering were soon overlaid by the Corona crisis. As Italy, whose economy was in trouble anyway, was also the first country of the western world to be affected by the pandemic, capital fled in droves. The capital flight went largely to Germany and caused the largest monthly change in Germany's Target balances ever since the outset of the Eurozone. Reacting to the crisis, huge fiscal and monetary rescue operations were set in place. If the crisis continues, the liquidity may flow back to Europe's seemingly safe havens in the north as has typically been the case throughout the euro crisis. The fiscal rescue funds would then have no significant effect on the Target balances of the Mediterranean countries as inflows and outflows would balance out, but the monetary rescue operations enabling NCBs to issue more liquidity would increase their Target debts.

11.1 The Pandemic Infects the World

With the Corona pandemic, a new phase in the development of the euro crisis began, as was argued in Chap. 5. The new crisis started in the medical sphere, but its necessary cure in terms of locking down large fractions of the population transformed it into an economic and financial crisis of unprecedented dimensions in the post-war period.

The disease began in Wuhan, China, a city of 11 million people, where a mutation of a virus harbored in wild animals, probably bats, had sprung over to humans in December 2019, if not earlier. The number of people infected and dying in Wuhan rose sharply during January 2020. After the Chinese New Year's festival (25 January), it was likely transported by hordes of tourists and guest workers from China to Italy, forcing the Italian government to ban flight connections with China on 30 January. It was also transported by single business contacts to Italy and a number of other places in Europe. The virus spread to neighboring countries, such as Spain, France and Austria, from where a large number of skiing tourists brought it to Germany. With a delay it ultimately reached the US through contacts with Asia and Europe. At this writing (25 April) the infection has killed about 200,000 people worldwide, among them 52,000 US Americans 26,000 Italians, 23,000 Spaniards, 22,000 French, 20,000 UK citizens and 6,000 Germans, and yet the virus is far from being under control. Epidemiologists forecast that the virus may recede a bit during the summer in the northern hemisphere but is likely to return in Winter 2020/2021, before it might be stopped with medication, vaccination and natural immunization.

The pandemic forced policy makers in most western countries to order a lock-down of their populations and reduce public life to a bare minimum in order to limit the death toll. The result is the worst economic crisis since World War II, even more severe than the Lehman crisis of 2008. At this stage, no one is able to make serious forecasts of the amount of economic contraction to be expected. Scenarios foresee decline at rates between 5% and, in the worst case, 20%.[1] 20% is a figure that reminds one of the Great Depression from 1929 to 1933, during which GDP in the US and other countries shrank by about 20% to 25%.[2] The IMF forecasts a severe recession of the world economy with a shrinkage rate of 3%, which is much worse than the "Great Recession" at the time of the Lehman crisis, which had a shrinkage rate of "only" 0.1%.[3] For the Eurozone, the IMF expects a recession with a shrinkage of 7.5%. The World Trade Organisation (WTO) forecasts that world trade will shrink by between 13% and 32% in 2020.[4]

Understandably, stock markets have been massively affected by the Corona shock. The European, American and European stock market indicators declined by nearly 40% within a month. This was not the largest decline in history, but the fastest decline for such a short period. Figure 11.1 compares the decline of the Dow Jones Index during the first weeks of the Corona crisis with the corresponding declines in previous crises down to the respective minima. It remains to be seen how the stock market will perform in the coming months. Much will depend on how fast the virus spreads in North America, where it arrived later than in Europe, and whether it will be possible for policy makers to limit the economic decline by sustaining economic activity with rescue programs and public demand management.

---

[1] See Dorn et al. (2020), Wollmershäuser (2020).
[2] See U.S. Department of Commerce (1975, pp. 224 and 232).
[3] See International Monetary Fund (2020b).
[4] See World Trade Organization (2020).

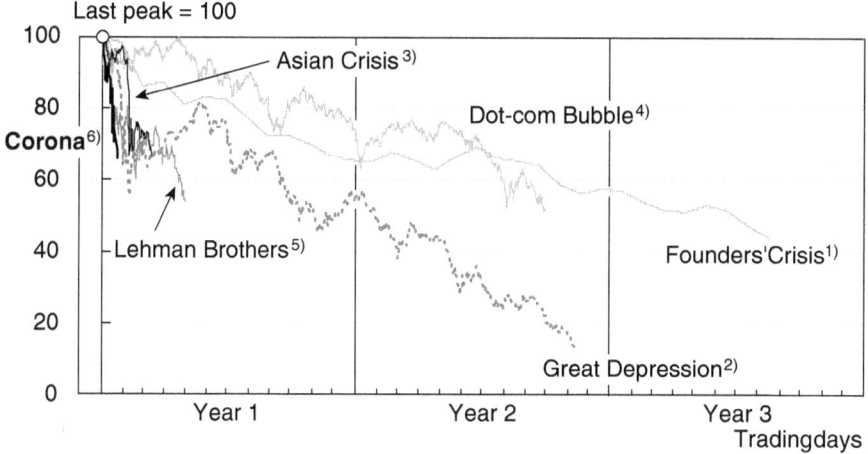

Fig. 11.1 Various stock market crashes in comparison. 1) Founders' Crisis, unweighted index of representative stocks, from March 1873, 2) Great Depression, S&P 500, from 16 September 1929, 3) Black Monday, Asian Crisis, S&P 500, from 21 August 1987, 4) Dot-com Bubble, S&P 500, from 24 March 2000, 5) Lehman Brothers, S&P 500, from 12 September 2008, 6) Corona crisis, S&P 500, from 19 February 2020. Note: Curves show the S&P-500 index curves based on trading days. The curve depicting the Founders' crisis is the index of stock market prices for Germany, an unweighted index of representative stocks, monthly data. Sources: Yahoo Finance, https://finance.yahoo.com/quote/%5EGSPC/history?period1=-1325462400&period2=1587081600&interval=1mo&filter=history&frequency=1mo, NBER Macrohistory: XI. Securities Markets, Germany, Index of Stock Prices 01/1870-12/1913, http://data.nber.org/databases/macrohistory/contents/chapter11.html, own calculations)

11.2 The Initial Impact of the Crisis on the Target Balances

A stock market crash results from an ultimately futile attempt of investors to flee from stocks into safe assets. The attempt is futile, as the volumes of outstanding stocks are given in the short run and cannot be changed by investors' decisions. What happens instead is that the attempt to flee causes stock prices to decline down to a point where investors give up their attempts.

But of course individual groups of investors are able to flee if other investors are willing to complement their trading offers and reshuffle their portfolios in the reverse direction. Such successful flight reactions may also involve the crossing of country borders in the Eurozone, and if they do, Target balances emerge. Thus, for example, an investor holding Italian government bonds may be able to sell these bonds to an Italian investor or institution, if only Banca d'Italia, makes a payment order to Germany, and buys German government bonds from a German investor who is willing to sell them. In this case, both the Italian Target debt and the German Target claim go up. Basically, it is now the Eurosystem that is willing to complement and enable the private capital flow from Italy to Germany with a countervailing public capital flow in the reverse direction as was explained in Chap. 2.

Indeed, Fig. 5.1 in Chap. 5 already showed that the Corona crisis resulted in a sharp increase in the Bundesbank's Target balances to € 935 billion in March 2020, the month during which the Corona crisis alarmed the entire world. With an amount of €114 billion, the increase was by far the largest since the start of the Eurozone.[5] The increase even exceeded the increase of €59 billion in September 2011 and of €69 billion in March 2012, which both characterized particularly tense periods of the euro crisis. The most important counterpart of Germany was Italy whose Target debt increased to €492 billion in March.

Again, however, the capital flight will likely have involved a large number of very different financial operations, not only the example cited. There may have been portfolio reallocations by investors from the Target creditor countries, from the Target debtor countries and from third countries. Or, because of their increasing mistrust in the Italian banking system, German banks may have wanted the money back they had lent to Italian banks after the ECB had incentivized such deals with its tiering decision. Alternatively, an Italian bank may have sold its government bonds to Banca d'Italia to lend the revenue to a German bank, and so on. These and similar operations all involve payment orders from Italy to Germany that increase both the respective Target debt and Target credit titles.

Surprisingly, Spain does not seem to have been the victim of capital flight this time. In March 2020, Spain's Target debt increased "only" by €15 billion reaching a value of €407 billion, while Italy's increased by €53 billion. This is very different from the years 2011 and 2012 when the capital flight from Spain and Italy had similar dimensions, as Fig. 5.1 revealed.

The reason why Italy accounted for the lion's share of capital flight presumably lies in the fact that it faced the double problem of not having been able to recover from the Lehman shock, with manufacturing output in Q4 being still 19% below the pre-crisis peak of Autumn 2007 (see Fig. 1.3), and of being the European epicenter of the Corona infection. The two problems are closely interlinked, as the textile industry's loss of competitiveness in the first decade of the euro had forced or induced Italian firms to resort to a mass import of cheap Chinese textile workers, which contributed to making Italy the European epicenter of the infection.

It is debatable to what extent the new surge in German and Italian Target balances resulted from the ECB's new asset purchases, the PEPP in particular. While these purchases distributed more liquidity to all European countries, the extra liquidity, which was not really needed for local transactions, may have been flowing to Germany for safety reasons. This would have been similar to the situation created by the ECB's QE program from Summer 2014 to the end

---

[5] This statement is based on the data sources given underneath Fig. 5.1 in Chap. 5. See also Sinn (2020).

of 2018 as reported in Chap. 8. The suspicion that the new asset purchases contributed to the new wave of capital flight is supported by the fact that, as Bloomberg reported,[6] the ECB deviated strongly from its self-imposed rule of buying government bonds in proportion to the national capital keys, allowing Banca d'Italia to go beyond the country limits.

However, for March, the direct effects of the asset purchases as such cannot have been very large as these purchases had only just started towards the end of the month. If anything, there might have been a speculative anticipation of measures yet to come, similar to the speculative anticipation effects observable before the QE decision of 2015 or before the tiering decision of 2019. Whatever the truth, the asset purchases are likely to have dominant effects on the Target balances in the following months, when the new programs succeed in channeling large quantities of money into the European economies.

The Target balances in that period will, however, also be strongly influenced by the fiscal rescue programs that, in the meantime, have been enacted.

11.3 The Rescue Measures

The Corona crisis caught policy makers by surprise, and it took them a while to understand what happened and how they could possibly react. While it seemed clear that quarantine measures would be appropriate, the correct economic reaction was not obvious. The difficulty in finding an adequate response was that the crisis was not characterized by people's unwillingness to buy, but by epidemiological constraints on transactions. People who would have liked to go shopping were prevented from doing so. Thus Keynesian demand management via deficit spending, which would operate by filling the shops, would clearly not be appropriate. Understandably, therefore, many countries resorted to fiscal rescue programs simply to save companies and banks from bankruptcy, so that they would be able to recover quickly once the pandemic was over.

For a similar reason, in countries with low social protection, pay checks were issued to low-income households to prevent personal bankruptcies and hardship. Others, like Germany, relied heavily on the automatic stabilization effect of their short-time work benefit schemes introduced during the Lehman crisis.

The largest fiscal rescue program has been set up in the US. After some hesitation, on 27 March 2020, the president signed a huge $2.2 trillion aid program involving nearly $900 billion lending to businesses, $600 billion direct payments and tax cuts, $300 billion expenses for social safety and unemployment insurance as well as payments for a number of smaller purposes.[7] The Congressional Budget Office (2020) predicted a public budget deficit of $3.7 trillion or 18% of US GDP in 2019, unparalleled in history. In the EU, the emphasis initially was more on individual programs. Thus, for example, Germany agreed at the federal level on a €156 billion supplementary budget

---

[6] See Skolimowski and Speciale (2020).
[7] See Snell (2020).

(4.9% of 2019 GDP) to cover medical expenses, short-time work compensation and grants to endangered firms. In addition, the federal government launched a €757 billion loan guarantees program for private firms, and the federal states implemented their own rescue programs reaching €48 billion in direct support and €63 billion in loan guarantees. Italy adopted a fiscal emergency package of €25 billion and unlocked government-backed guarantees of €750 billion to facilitate borrowing from banks. France so far provided €100 billion fiscal stimulus and state guarantees of €312 billion.[8]

In addition, however, on the Summit of 23 April 2020, the EU countries agreed to a €540 billion program, of which €100 will be for funding a new EU short-time work compensation scheme, €240 billion will come from the rescue fund ESM to support government budgets and €200 will be provided by the European Investment Bank as credit to private firms.[9] On top of that, a discussion about expanding the EU budget and establishing a huge European reconstruction fund prevailed, again involving hundreds of billions of euros, perhaps even more than a trillion.

The announcements of the programs initiated in the US and Europe mitigated the economic panic and rebooted the stock markets. It is hoped that this will be enough to bring central parts of the world economy back to normal in a few months after the lock-down is gradually loosened. However, the risk of a double dip recession in the fight against a possibly resistant and mutating virus persists.

Both in the US and in Europe, it is expected that the lions' shares of the fiscal funds specified above will ultimately come from the printing presses. Thus, the Federal Reserve Bank (2020) announced on 9 April that it intends to extend its credit provision and asset purchases with freshly printed dollars in the order of $2.2 trillion, providing loans to enterprises and co-financing the government program. And, as was mentioned in the last chapter, the ECB has established its €750 billion Pandemic Emergency Purchase Programme (PEPP) involving the purchase of government bonds, bonds of rescue programs and private bonds.[10] Together with the other measures that it had already agreed on before, this program will bring its overall expenses of freshly printed money in 2020 to €1.1 trillion.[11] Never before has the ECB spent so much money on asset purchases in such a short period of time. In addition, the ECB tried to activate refinancing operations by again dramatically reducing its collateral requirements along the lines it did in the first phase of the euro crisis, as was described in Chap. 5.[12] It even decided to admit collaterals that the rating

---

[8] Figures refer to as of 10 April 2020. See International Monetary Fund (2020a).
[9] See Michel (2020) and Eurogroup (2020).
[10] European Central Bank (2020a).
[11] European Central Bank (2020c). The sum includes €20 billion regular monthly asset purchases, an addition € 120 billion envelope for potential asset purchases decided on 12 March and the €750 billion PEPP.
[12] See European Central Bank (2020b).

agencies would classify as "no-investment grade",[13] thus increasing the probability that the collateral would be insufficient to safeguard its lending in a crisis.

All of these measures will affect the Target balances, but not in the same way. While the purchases of government bonds by the respective NCBs as well as the reduction of collateral requirements will increase the Target imbalances, as explained, the other measures will, at least in the first instance, reduce them, given that they will mostly involve liquidity flows from the international capital market via the EU's fiscal rescue funds towards the crisis-inflicted countries in southern Europe. It is unclear, however, whether this extra liquidity arriving in the territories of the Target debtor countries will remain there or whether an ongoing crisis will again mean that all central bank money not urgently needed for domestic transactions will flow to the safe havens, i.e. the Target creditor countries. In this case there would be no major net effects on the Target balances from the flow of liquidity via the fiscal rescue funds, and the outflow of liquidity stemming from the NCBs' purchases of local government bonds and from lowered collateral requirements for refinancing credit would prevail, increasing the imbalances.

It is too early, however, to fully understand what will happen, as capital markets and policy makers are extremely nervous as of this writing. A few days before the manuscript of this book was completed, French President Emmanuel Macron argued, in an interview with the Financial Times, that the very existence of the Eurozone was at risk, and he was close to formulating an ultimatum to mobilize more funds for the countries most affected by the Corona crisis (including presumably France).[14] It is unlikely that this will be the last word in Europe's ongoing euro tragedy, but whatever a later observation of the then-available data will reveal, the Target balances will be part of the emerging picture.

---

[13] See European Central Bank (2020c).
[14] Macron (2020).

CHAPTER 12

The Risks of Target and Cash Balances

Given that a country's Target and cash balances claims have resulted from a delivery of goods and assets to other countries and are serviced with intra-Eurosystem interest, a total or partial loss of these claims would imply a real resource loss of its state and its taxpayers. The loss can happen if a country leaves the Eurozone, if the Eurozone breaks up or if the Target debtor country's banks and government default. In the first case, the remaining Eurosystem may lose its Target and cash claims on the leaving country, and the single NCBs remaining in the Eurosystem would then share the losses in proportion to their sizes (paid-in capital keys). In the second case, the internal quota system may become void and each single creditor NCB may lose its respective national Target and cash claim. In the third case, the Eurosystem may effectively lose its entire Target and cash balance claims against the defaulting country even when the statutory standard case of no risk sharing applies, because the respective NCB may become insolvent internally with regard to the Eurosystem. This possibility is unrelated to the fact that an NCB may operate with negative equity capital and that the Eurosystem cannot become insolvent with regard to the non-central bank sectors. The variety of risks creates a powerful threat point for over-indebted countries to urge other member countries to help out with fiscal transfers, debt mutualization and Target credit. Thus, the ECB's Governing Council rather than the parliaments may eventually decide Europe's path towards fiscal unification.

12.1 Target and Cash Balances were Built Up in Exchange for Goods and Assets

In view of the enormous magnitude of the German Target claims, exceeding its central government budget by far and approaching half of its entire net foreign asset position, the question has been asked whether the Target claims would

---

The original version of this chapter was revised. The correction to this chapter can be found at https://doi.org/10.1007/978-3-030-50170-9_14

involve budgetary risks and if so, under what conditions these risks might emerge. As already explained, there is a popular faction of politicians and even some scholars who—if only because they are afraid of the political implications of a Target debate—argue that the Target and cash balances are irrelevant and meaningless clearing items of the Eurosystem. If, for whatever reason, they ceased to exist, nothing would be lost to the creditor countries. At a higher level of sophistication, this statement is sometimes justified by maintaining that the balances did not result from a credit relationship, that they cannot be called due, and that they do not bear any interest. It has already been shown that only the second of these statements is true while the other two are wrong. Target and cash balances measure loans between NCBs and the Eurosystem, and they effectively generate interest through the pooling of seignorage. And even if they cannot be called due, they can still be repaid by the debtor countries selling goods and securities with an identical present value, discounted at the effective rate of interest that was calculated with Eq. (9.12). The valuation of the Target balances as assets and liabilities in the NCBs' balance sheets and in the Eurostat accounting system is therefore basically correct.

Target and cash balance claims have arisen in exchange for valuable objects in the sense of goods and assets, both being broadly defined. The goods include everything reported in the current account, and the assets include company shares, real estate, government bonds, bonds, bank accounts and private debentures, but also the securitized and non-securitized debt titles that were bought back or redeemed as well as NCB deposits built up by large international investment banks. Chapter 8 laid out that the latter was a temporary phenomenon of very limited importance though. As was shown in Chaps. 5 and 6, in the first phase of the crisis, Target and cash balance credits were used by the debtors primarily for the acquisition of goods, for debt redemption and for genuine foreign investment.[1] And as argued in Chap. 8, the rising Target balances since 2014 instead resulted primarily from the repurchase of government bonds by the NCBs under the PSPP. Finally, in the Corona crisis of 2020, they resulted from a panic portfolio reallocation towards countries considered to be safe havens, which also involved the exchange of assets for Target balances.

From the viewpoint of the Target and cash balance creditor countries, this development is not without risk. If valuable objects never came back for the delivery of goods and assets and if not even interest was transferred in the form of such objects, the countries that made the deliveries would suffer a permanent real loss of wealth, negatively affecting the long-term living standard of their populations, while the reverse would be true in the debtor countries receiving the goods and assets.

Had it been known from the outset that nothing would ever return, the creditor NCBs would not have been able to activate their Target and cash balances in their balance sheets. By now they would have accumulated losses at the expense of their owners, the respective nation states, equal to these balances. In the case of the Bundesbank, this would have meant not recording, or writing

---

[1] Sinn (2014a, chapter 7) provided an extensive analysis for most Eurozone countries.

off ex post, €459.455 billion up to the end of 2019. Since the sum of the Bundesbank's equity (capital and reserves, €5.720 billion)) and the valuation reserves (revaluation accounts, €144.220 billion) at the end of 2019 was €149.940 billion, the Bundesbank's equity capital would have turned negative to €-309.515 billion.

From a purely operational point of view this would not necessarily be a problem, because an NCB that lost intra-Eurosystem interest on its Target and cash balance claims may still enjoy primary seignorage income from its lending to the local economy. Clearly any of the world's central banks can operate with negative equity capital as long as it owns "seignorage wealth" in the sense of the present value of its interest claims against the rest of the economy.

However, from an economic point of view, there would be a loss in terms of the lost seignorage wealth and the present value of consumption that tax payers ultimately would have been able to buy with this wealth. Moreover, in the opinion of the European Central Bank, the NCB whose equity becomes negative would have to be recapitalized by the respective state to conduct its business properly.[2] The German Constitutional Court also shares this opinion, arguing that the German state would be obliged to recapitalize the Bundesbank should its equity turn negative because it bears an "institutional burden" (*Anstaltslast*).[3]

The simplest way to carry out such a recapitalization is filling up the missing accounting equity capital with government bonds given to the NCBs, which would increase the government debt accordingly. If we apply this rule to Germany's situation at the end of 2019, the Bundesbank would need a gift of government bonds equal to €309.515 billion plus the normal amount of capital and reserves, €5.720 billion. This sum would increase the German debt/GDP ratio from 61% to around 72%, which is much more than the 60% maximum that the Maastricht Treaty allows.[4]

But this is not the way things are. Indeed, the accounting systems of the Eurozone and the EU report the Target and cash balances in their net foreign asset positions and their increase in the balance of payment account in a similar way as private foreign investment. The creditor countries therefore can still hope that one day goods or marketable assets will return for what they once delivered. And not only that, given the way the Eurosystem organizes the pooling of seignorage, they can also hope to receive compound interest, since this is piling up in the Target system.

---

[2] See European Central Bank (2016d, p. 25/26): "Therefore, the event of an NCB's net equity becoming less than its statutory capital or even negative would require that the respective member state provides the NCB with an appropriate amount of capital at least up to the level of the statutory capital within a reasonable period of time so as to comply with the principle of financial independence."

[3] See Bundesverfassungsgericht (2016, no. 217, 2017, no. 126).

[4] See Treaty on the Functioning of the European Union (TFEU), Article 126 and Protocol (No 12) on the excessive deficit procedure, Article 1. The calculation is based on the published public debt figure as of third quarter of 2019.

The only question is how justified this hope is. How great are the risks that the Target and cash claims of the creditor countries will be lost and on what do these risks depend? That is the question that will be examined in this chapter.

12.2 Exit Risks, Exemplified by the Case of Italy

If a country leaves the euro area and does not respect its Target and cash balance debts and the resulting payment obligations in the course of interest pooling, then the debts will not be repaid. The assets and goods for which foreign NCBs acquired the corresponding claims are gone, and nothing comes back.[5]

The country that is in the center of attention in these considerations is Italy. Italy's exit from the euro area is not impossible. As was mentioned before, former minister president Silvio Berlusconi conducted secret negotiations about the exit of his country in the autumn of 2011, but was forced to resign once that became known to the Italian establishment and the EU.[6] Nevertheless, the issue remains virulent in Italy, because the Lega under Matteo Salvini in 2017 campaigned with the threat of leaving, and when it had won the elections in 2018 and formed a coalition government with Cinque Stelle, another party that had popped up recently, its finance spokESMan, Claudio Borghi, repeatedly emphasized that Italy must consider exiting the euro.[7] In May 2019, he even managed to persuade the Italian Parliament to unanimously prepare for the introduction of a parallel currency (mini-BOTs)[8] a plan that had been developed by Italy's Minister of European Affairs Paolo Savona. The presentation of this plan created uproar in Brussels because it was rightly understood as an exit preparation.[9] The coalition's failure and the formation of a new government in 2019 initially put the issue on hold, but the Lega became even stronger in the polls, which makes it not unlikely that Italy will further pursue these plans in the foreseeable future. The fact that Italy's economy is being further severely hit by the Corona crisis having afflicted the country more and earlier than all other European economies does not improve this assessment.

In 2017, former ECB President Draghi was asked by two MEPs from the Cinque Stelle party, which did not approve of the idea of exiting the euro, how their country's Target debts should be treated if they were to leave. Draghi (2017) replied with a detailed explanation of the Target balances and closed his

---

[5] The point was made many times in the author's early writings, the earliest statement being Sinn (2011b). With arguments that showed some similarity with the Modern Monetary Theory, it was disputed by De Grauwe and Ji (2012), whose view in turn was rejected by Sinn (2012d). Cf. also Sinn (2012a, c, pp. 275–78, 2014a, pp. 265f, 2015b, pp. 363–66, 2018b, c). A similar debate later emerged when Hellwig (2018a, b) as well as Hellwig and Schnabel (2019) again expressed the view that the Target balances are irrelevant accounting items whose loss would be be meaningless. Hellwig's views were refuted by Homburg (2019b), Spahn (2019), van Suntum (2019) and Sinn (2019b).

[6] Compare Bini Smaghi (2013, p. 29).

[7] See, e.g. Borghi (2019).

[8] Italian Parliament (2019).

[9] See Gros (2018).

letter by stating that Italy would have to fully settle its liabilities to the Eurosystem in the event of an exit:[10]

> Se un paese lasciasse l'Eurosistema, i crediti e le passività della sua banca centrale nazionale nei confronti della Bce dovrebbero essere regolati integralmente.

However, what would happen if a country exits the Eurosystem is not explicitly specified in the ECB's bylaws, let alone the EU treaties. Thus, Mario Draghi's answer may be legally on somewhat shaky ground. It was probably provoked by Cinque Stelle to counter the strategic games played by the Lega. The Lega in turn seemed to calculate that Italy would be able to get rid of the Target debt if it left. Be that as it may, it follows from the style of the letter that the ECB regards the Target and cash balances as valuable and their loss as financial damage for the countries remaining in the Eurosystem. Italy's Target balances were −€439 billion by the end of 2019, and its cash balances were +€44 billion. Thus its overall Target and cash balance debt was €395 billion. If it left the Eurozone without settling this debt, Germany would lose 32% or €125 billion, France 25% or €97 billion, the Netherlands 7% or €28 billion, Finland 2% or €9 billion, Belgium 4% or €17 billion and Greece 3% or €12 billion, just to take a few examples. The percentages mentioned are the respective countries' shares in the paid-in capital of the ECB after Italy's share (17%) is deducted.[11]

Whilst these are substantial magnitudes, there could be a further loss item if it is not possible to collect the bank notes circulating in Italy or to completely devalue them at the time of exit. If Italians continue to be able to use the euro banknotes they own to buy goods and assets from the remaining Eurozone countries, these goods and assets would be gone while the citizens remaining in the Eurozone would merely get the euro paper that their NCBs could equally well have printed for them at negligible cost if there were any use for the extra liquidity.

However, such an assumption would have an ad hoc character without any justification. If the ECB optimized its monetary policy, whatever the specific goals are that it pursues, the extra liquidity returning from the exiting economy in exchange for valuables would probably have to be destroyed by a contractionary monetary policy. This would permanently reduce the seignorage income from lending this liquidity out to the private sector of the remaining euro NCBs, inducing a wealth loss for tax payers equal to the amount of bank notes returning from Italy.

The collection of banknotes from Italians in order to avoid these losses is technically impossible. People would hide their banknotes somewhere and

---

[10] Author's translation: "If a country leaves the Eurosystem, its national central bank's claims and liabilities to the ECB would have to be settled in full."

[11] The percentages are the paid-in capital shares divided by one minus the Italian paid-in capital share.

would secretly try to bring them out of the country, an attempt that the Mafia would happily support at reasonable fees.

The only way to avoid the losses would be devaluing all old euro bank notes and exchanging them for new ones, while excluding Italian citizens. However, even if officials tried to keep this secret and capital controls were introduced, many people would succeed in preemptively smuggling bank notes out of the country and exchanging them into foreign currencies. Capital controls would be unavoidable but hardly effective. A massive devaluation of the euro exchange rate would result. Given the difficulties with such a solution, there will likely be a further loss to euro citizens up to the statutory amount of bank notes in circulation $\bar{B}_i$ (see Chaps. 7 and 9) if Italy left the Eurozone. By the end of 2019, this would have been €202 billion according to Banca d'Italia's balance sheet.

Together with Italy's Target liability (€439 billion) and its cash balance claim (€44 billion), there would hence be an overall loss for the rest of the Eurozone equal to €597 billion if Italy actually left, if it did not respect its obligations under the Eurosystem and if the Eurosystem were unable to destroy or devalue the bank notes circulating in Italy. Germany's share would be €190 billion and France's €147 billion.[12]

12.3 Risks of a Euro Break-Up

Target balances have been discussed intensely in Germany, because Germany is by far the largest Target creditor, and the German public is concerned about the potential risks involved. The Bundesbank rightly tried to calm down these fears by emphasizing that when a country leaves the Eurozone, "the amount of the German TARGET2 balance or the Bundesbank's net claims on the ECB are irrelevant" for the potential losses of Germany, as the losses would be shared by the remaining Eurozone members.[13] It is indeed irrelevant how the Target claims and liabilities are distributed across the remaining countries of the Eurozone, unless the ECB Governing Council decides that the write-off losses be distributed in relation to the NCB's Target and cash balances. While the internal rules of the Eurosystem are silent about what would happen in the case of an exit, it is, however, reasonable to predict that the exit losses would be treated like other losses and be shared in proportion to the paid-in capital keys.

It would be different though if the Eurosystem as such broke up. In such a case, the ECB's bylaws would cease to exist. It is entirely unclear what would happen in this case. A plausible forecast is that the cash circulating in each country as well as the banks' deposits with the NCB would be exchanged for

---

[12] See Homburg (2019a) for similar calculations. In the event of a Greek exit, Sinn (2014a, pp. 349–51, 2015b, pp. 490f.) suggested allowing Greece to keep the euro cash circulating there, so as not to have to exchange all banknotes, assigning the country a corresponding government debt with the Eurozone instead.

[13] Deutsche Bundesbank (2019, p. 17). This is in line with the very first calculation of Bundesbank risks by Sinn (2011b).

the respective new currency, while the Target and cash balance creditor countries would be unable to collect their claims, given that they are directed to a system that no longer exists. It is hard to imagine, for example, that the debtor NCBs would be prepared to respect the creditors' claims by transferring interest-bearing debt instruments or other valuable assets to them, given that even some economists of the creditor countries had declared the Target and cash balance claims irrelevant items. It is more likely in this case that the creditor NCBs would maintain their claims and defiantly keep them as assets in their balances sheets. However, as the pooling of seignorage would halt, there would be no intra-Eurosystem interest payments any more on the balance sheet claims. That would devalue these claims completely from an economic perspective.

Fortunately for the creditor countries, unlike the case of single exits, there would be no further losses due to the amounts of currency in circulation ($\bar{B}_i$), because if the entire system collapsed, the old bank notes could not be used to make purchases in other countries. Each former member state would instead devalue them, making equal per-capita gifts with new bank notes to its citizens or converting the old bank notes into new ones only for domestic citizens.

However, there is a danger that goes beyond the loss of the balances insofar as in the crisis that would likely precede the collapse of the Eurosystem, a great amount of money, in expectation of revaluation gains, would probably be sent to the stronger countries of the Eurozone like the Netherlands and Germany. There would be a last minute capital flight, before the payment orders are stopped by capital controls, increasing the Target balances in exchange for real resources leaving these countries. Thus the potential losses for the Target creditor countries would be substantially bigger than what the current Target balances suggest.

This would also be true for banknotes that might physically be transported to these countries to buy assets that are protected from devaluation losses. The extra cash would not affect the cash balance as it is defined and calculated, given that this is based on the fiction that the statutory amount of bank notes in circulation $\bar{B}_i$ is the actual amount in circulation (see Chaps. 4 and 7). Nevertheless, in the strong countries it would involve a loss very similar to the loss resulting from higher Target balances because their NCBs would probably have to exchange the euros stemming from other Eurozone countries into new domestic currencies like any other cash that its citizens present.

12.4 Risks without Exits

It is often argued that Target balances only represent a risk if a country leaves the Eurozone or if the Eurosystem collapses and is dissolved, and as this will not happen, no one should be concerned.[14] Unfortunately, this argument is not correct. In fact, there are risks even if no country leaves, because, as is the

---

[14] See, for example, Krahnen (2018).

case with ordinary obligations, the Target and cash balance claims are subject to a normal default risk. This has been shown by Fuest and Sinn (2018a, b) for the case where the liquidity shift measured by the balances is only compensated with changes in local money creation credits while leaving bank deposits untouched.[15]

To understand and generalize the argument, suppose first that the NCBs granted money creation credits (refinancing loans given to banks and securities purchased by NCBs) in joint liability. In this case, all euro countries would share in NCB i's losses from the default of private and public debtors according to their paid-in capital keys anyway, and obviously, not only the Target and cash balances would be at risk.

Let us concentrate, however, on the statutory standard case that each NCB is liable for the money creation credits it has granted itself and risk sharing is formally excluded. (This was explained and discussed in Box 9.1 in Chap. 9.) Interestingly enough, even in this case the Eurosystem is not fully protected against the failure of NCB i's assets, if this NCB has a Target and cash liability. It can be shown that NCB i now can become insolvent within the Eurozone and impose a loss on the other members of the Eurosystem equal to the sum of their Target and cash balances vis-à-vis the defaulting economy. The proof is not trivial because, as was mentioned above, from a purely economic point of view, an NCB in principle may operate with negative equity without becoming insolvent.

The proof can be given for arbitrary structures of sources and sinks of liquidity in the framework of the model set up in Chap. 9.[16] Let us assume that the economy of NCB i, which has a substantial Target and cash balance liability, collapses. Private securities owned by NCB i are no longer serviced, the local government goes bankrupt and with it the local banking system, whose balance sheet is loaded with government bonds, which is a typical problem in the Eurozone. This will be a major problem for NCB i, because commercial banks are their most important debtors and government bonds their most important securities.[17] In such a situation NCB i can no longer collect the primary interest income that it normally earns on its monetary aggregates according to Eq. (9.6) in Chap. 9, and it can no longer transfer it to the common seignorage pool.

---

[15] See also Fuest and Sinn (2015, 2016, 2018b, pp. 32–34). A numerical example, which shows that in the event of a bankruptcy of a national financial system without exits, the Target balances, and only the Target balance, are lost, can be found in one of the texts I wrote for the macro discussion group organized by C. C. von Weizsäcker (Sinn 2018c). The argument goes back to Sinn (2015a, b, Box 8.1, pp. 383f.).

[16] This exposition follows Sinn (2019a).

[17] Krahnen (2019) countered Fuest and Sinn (2018a, b) claiming that the regulation of banks is so good today that NCB's money creation loans can no longer fail, as these authors had assumed. Fuest and Sinn (2019) replied that the monetary assets of an NCB today mainly contain government bonds and other securities that cannot be made secure by bank regulation, as the banks are not the debtors. Moreover, they doubted whether the banking regulation would provide adequate protection for refinancing loans.

Note that, as shown above, the transfer of interest takes the form of writing down an additional Target liability only. Thus, in order to "pay" the intra-Eurosystem interest on Target and cash balances, the debtor NCB does not really need any primary interest income from the domestic economy. The interest is simply recorded in the Target system, and it may seem at first glance that this can go on with compound interest forever. However, as was demonstrated, non-zero Target and cash balances do have immediate implications for the distribution of central bank liquidity among the associated economies. These consequences limit the process because they can affect monetary policy and the orderly business of the Eurosystem.

To show this, let us make the simplifying assumption of full symmetry in the average and marginal structure of monetary aggregates in country i and the rest of the Eurozone $i*$.[18] This implies that there is no intra-Eurosystem redistribution of seignorage between economy i and the rest of the Eurozone, $i*$, when there are no Target and cash balances, and that such redistribution can only arise because such balances occur. The overall amount of base money and seignorage revenue stay unaffected by the balances when there are no bankruptcies. Assume the absence of bankruptcies for a moment, before we can see what happens when the bankruptcies occur.

If there are no bankruptcies, pooling would force economy i to transfer the extra primary seignorage it earns because of its initial negative Target and cash balance to the other NCBs $i*$ whose initial Target and cash balance is positive, compensating for their loss of primary seignorage income from which these NCBs suffer due to the initial liquidity inflow.[19] As each NCB has a share α_j, $j = i, i*$, in the aggregate seignorage that is proportional to its size, neither NCB i's seignorage nor that of the rest of the Eurozone $i*$ changes. As was shown, this implies the transfer of effective intra-Eurosystem interest on the Target and cash balances from i to $i*$, which then leads to a secondary increase in the Target balances. (NCB i's intra-Eurosystem interest payment is recorded as an additional Target liability and the intra-Eurosystem interest received by NCBs $i*$ is recorded as an additional Target claim.) NCBs $i*$ can now distribute to "their" states not only the reduced primary interest income that they draw from their economies after the liquidity measured by the Target and cash balances has flown in, but also the compensating intra-Eurosystem interest stemming from country i. NCB i, in turn, cannot distribute all its primary interest to the domestic state, because the part that originated from the negative initial Target and cash balances has to be delivered to the pool. Thus the increase of primary seignorage income in the debtor country i and the decrease

---

[18] Note that unlike in the previous chapters i now stands for a particular debtor country and $i*$ for the aggregate of the creditor countries, because the analysis focuses on a single country's bankruptcy.

[19] Recall that a reduction of Target and cash balances implies more interest revenue for the local NCB, because banks need more money creation credit, or less interest expenses, because banks hold larger deposits with the NCB, while the reverse is true with the other NCBs. For details see Chap. 9.

of primary seignorage income in the creditor countries i^* that both originate from the initial Target and cash balances imply a shift of income and liquidity from the debtor to the creditor economy. All of this was discussed in detail in Chap. 9.

Assume now that the institutions of country i become insolvent in the sense explained (government, banks, securities). In this case the withdrawal of liquidity and income that goes along with the transfer of intra-Eurosystem interest can no longer take place. There are two possibilities as to how the Eurosystem can react.

The first is that the Governing Council decides on a debt relief, thus acknowledging the bankruptcy of NCB i. No intra-Eurosystem seignorage transfer is booked in the Target balances, and hence NCBs i^* and their respective owner-states suffer permanently from lower profits. The taxpayers in i^* will bear the losses in full. The present value of these losses is equal to the initial Target and cash balances. Fair value accounting would imply that these balances be written off immediately after the bankruptcy occurred.

The second possibility is that the Eurosystem simply keeps booking the secondary Target balances arising from the intra-Eurosystem interest payments as additional liabilities and claims as if nothing had happened. This would shield the other countries, i^*, from any immediate effect of the bankruptcies in country i. NCBs i^* would be able to distribute as much profit to the respective states as without these bankruptcies, given that they would anyway produce the necessary liquidity themselves. Nevertheless, less seignorage and hence less liquidity and income is extracted from economy i than would have been the case without the bankruptcies, simply because the bankrupt institutions do not deliver the base money which therefore keeps circulating in the non-central bank sector. Thus, the aggregate stock of base money of the Eurosystem is now increasing, while normally with the symmetry assumptions about sources and sinks of liquidity flows it would not increase if Target and cash balances emerge.

Prima facie, the bankruptcy of economy i does not hurt anyone else, given that all agents in economies i^*, including NCBs, states and tax payers still receive the same money and earn the same income as before. Modern Monetary Theory (MMT) maintains that the bankruptcies do not affect the rest of the Eurozone economy. Printing money generates resources from thin air. However, it should not be forgotten that this would violate the ECB's monetary policy goals and imply a different inflation rate than the one the Governing Council was aiming at. The functioning of the Eurosystem would be impaired if this process were allowed to proceed.

There is agreement in mainstream economics that the arguments of the MMT are not analytically acceptable.[20] Given a monetary policy for the euro area that has been found to be correct, NCB i's inability to withdraw interest from its own insolvent economy by necessity requires that the creditor NCBs

---

[20] See Rogoff (2019) who speaks of "Modern Monetary Nonsense" or Summers (2019) who considers this theory to be the "voodoo economics of our time".

i^* cannot distribute the interest on their Target and cash balances to their respective states either, even if this were legally possible. This is what could be called the *economic insolvency* of a national central bank in a currency union.[21]

Normally a company is bankrupt when its losses exceed its equity capital, turning it negative, or, equivalently, when the loss of annual returns exceeds the normal annual return on its equity capital. This is not so with central banks, because they earn seignorage from the monetary aggregates which involve assets that they produced themselves without cost. However, although a central bank's equity may become negative, the present value of its seignorage income is usually a limit for the extent to which it may become negative.[22]

The NCBs in the Eurozone are no exception. Accordingly, NCB i, in addition to the return on its equity capital, is entitled to receive its fair share of the annual seignorage income of the Eurozone. Bankruptcy would therefore only occur if NCB i's loss in primary seignorage income—whose normal return it has to deliver to the seignorage pool regardless of whether or not it actually earns it—exceeds its share in the secondary seignorage income it receives from this pool plus the return on its equity capital.

Under the symmetry assumptions made, this is not possible if there is no Target and cash balance liability. If the balance is zero, the secondary interest income returned from the pool is as large as the amount of seignorage that NCB i has to deliver to the pool, and hence it can, despite the bankruptcies, just fulfill its obligations by pledging what comes back from the pool at the expense of its owner state. NCB i therefore in principle could stay solvent even if its own interest losses exceed the return on its equity capital.[23]

Things are very different, though, when there are Target and cash liabilities. In this case, pledging the secondary seignorage returning from the pool is not enough to fulfill the delivery obligations because the liquidity outflow measured by the negative Target and cash balances required additional refinancing credit or lower deposits which all increase the primary seignorage income that needs to be delivered to the pool. Now, the only income possibly remaining in the case of economy i's bankruptcy could stem from NCB i's equity and the assets behind it. However, if the entire economy collapses, these assets will likely also fail. Thus NCB i can no longer meet its obligations from a proper course of business, because it is economically insolvent.

---

[21] This is the core idea of the contributions by Fuest and Sinn (2015, 2016, 2018a, b) and Sinn (2015a), where it was shown that the Target and cash balances in Greece already far exceeded the possible limit for self-liability.

[22] In a dynamic setting, this limit is higher by the present value of additional seignorage that in the future can be collected from a growing stock of money balances.

[23] In any case, NCB i would always be solvent if there was a statutory joint liability of all central banks for all money creation assets, but, as explained in section 9, such a joint liability is not foreseen by the statutes and not considered here either, notwithstanding occasional mutualization decisions of the Governing Council. It is therefore assumed that NCB i will have to pay interest to the pool at the main refinancing rate even if it itself does not generate any interest from its assets. This applies to ELA, ANFA and PSPP as well as to other forms of money creation loans.

A possible objection to this result is that an insolvency is impossible because the local state would have to recapitalize its central bank to ensure its smooth operation. However, this argument does not apply in the case at hand because the state itself is assumed to be bankrupt, triggering the internal insolvency of its NCB. The state clearly would not be able to collect the means necessary for recapitalization.

Thus, the view cited at the outset that negative Target and cash balances will only be able to impose a risk on the rest of the Eurozone i^* if the respective country exits is clearly not true. The existence of negative balances implies uncovered risks even if the Eurosystem remains intact and the economy of the debtor NCB encounters difficulties such that its institutions are unable to service their debts. These difficulties transfer directly to the others' risk of losing their Target and cash balance claims on this economy.

12.5 The Blackmailing Potential of Target and Cash Balances and the Dutch Disease

It has been argued that all of this risk sharing implicit in the Target and cash balances is of minor importance, given that creditor countries might have to reckon with further losses in the event of the collapse of a major Eurozone economy, a euro exit or even the collapse of the entire Eurosystem because, due to potential export surpluses in the past, their citizens are likely to hold a large number of private foreign assets that would also be subject to severe losses, be they losses from a currency devaluation or bankruptcies. However, these additional losses do not reduce the concern about the potential loss of the Target and cash balance claims, but increase them. After all, it is one of the fundamental assumptions of economics that the marginal disutility from damages tends to increase with the amount of damages. The view that additional losses are easier to cope with when some losses are already there has no basis in economic thinking.

All of this is not meant to say that catastrophes of the kind analyzed in this chapter are likely or imminent. The problem with the break-up scenario is not its likelihood but its implicit blackmailing potential. To avoid the Target and cash balance losses and the resulting political turmoil, the creditor countries may well be willing to sacrifice real resources in a creeping piecemeal fashion that stays below the threshold of public attention. Thus, the creditor countries might agree to public transfers and guarantees that undermine their financial autonomy and the living standard of their citizens. Examples are the credit default insurance that came with the ECB's OMT program, a common Eurozone deposit insurance (EDIS) protecting the customers of insecure banks, and sharing unemployment risks of countries that lost their competitiveness in the pre-Lehman bubble and so on. Other examples are the various bail-out activities of the ECB including negative interest rates and asset purchase programs that all create artificial revaluation gains that makes debt finance easy for over-indebted firms, institutions and states. The range of possibilities also includes the European fiscal union with explicit redistribution goals that President Macron (2017) called for in his Sorbonne speech and that he reiterated rigorously on 16 April in the interview with the Financial Times cited at the outset of the previous chapter. The higher the total of a NCB's Target and cash balances, the more generous the respective owner-state must be when granting fiscal guarantees and aid funds for the financially stricken countries of the Eurozone.

This is not only problematic because it turns democracy on its head, but also because it preserves the loss of competitiveness from which the southern countries of the Eurozone suffer as was explained and shown at the outset of this book (see Chap. 1, Fig. 1.3). The more public and private funds are redirected into the debtor countries that lost their competitiveness in the pre-euro bubble, the stronger are the forces that prevent a correction of wrong relative prices and the larger is the risk that these countries will be driven into a permanent Dutch disease.

The Dutch disease is a term that characterizes the Dutch economy in the 1960s and 1970s.[24] After the Netherlands discovered natural gas on its territory, the proceeds from selling the gas allowed domestic wage increases that made the economy too expensive and undermined the competitiveness of the manufacturing sector. Borrowed and given funds coming from other countries in principle have the same implications. They increase the living standard but keep the recipient countries too expensive for exactly that reason. This undermines the competitiveness of the existing manufacturing sector and prevents new industrial settlements from being established. Other examples of the Dutch disease include the Italian Mezzogiorno[25] and Germany's new eastern states.[26] The latter two suffered from a combination of wage standards determined by other parts of the economy (the north in Italy, the west in Germany) and transfers through the public budget that sustain the living standard despite the devastating consequences of overblown wages.

Thus the policy of perpetual firefighting with the means of the ECB which have created the Target and cash balances of the Eurozone has successfully prevented the collapse of the Eurozone, but at the same time is threatening to drive the Target debtor countries in the Mediterranean sphere into a situation of permanent stagnation. Although the living standard is successfully sustained in such a sate, the recipient economies will always remain dependent, suffer from high unemployment and never again become an attractive investment location.

---

[24] See Corden and Neary (1982).
[25] See Sinn and Westermann (2001).
[26] See Sinn and Sinn (1992).

CHAPTER 13

Conclusions and Policy Recommendations

Target overdraft credit in principle is a useful shock absorber in the case of liquidity and confidence crises that entail the risk of fire sales and capital flight. However, as it may grow without bounds and does not have to be settled, it also enables the ECB to depress the interest spreads among European countries below the levels implied by differences in creditworthiness, which would induce less prudent and parsimonious financial behavior than otherwise would be the case.

To balance the pros and cons of the Target system, a staggered system of brackets with progressively rising penalty interest for the Target and cash balances is recommended, so as to induce local NCBs to react less elastically to liquidity outflows and tolerate local interest increases that would reduce these outflows. This system could be reinforced by introducing voting in proportion to the paid-in capital key in the ECB's Governing Council, by a broadening of the ECB's mandate to avoid balance-of-payments disequilibria as well as by introducing annual gold settlement for the balances following rules that prevailed with the US "District Feds" until 1975. Later, when the EU may have transformed into a political union, the settlement system could be relaxed to settlement with marketable assets such as the one prevailing in the US today.

13.1 The Findings of This Book

This book has dealt with the weighty topic of Target and cash balances in the Eurozone and has explained what they mean and why they came about. A country's Target balance measures the stock of net international payment orders fulfilled by its national central bank (NCB), and its cash balance attempts to measure the stock of euro banknotes that flowed in in net terms from abroad and is now circulating at home. The Target and cash balances can be seen as international public overdraft loans, because they indicate open, unsecured positions credited by the domestic NCB, enabling the net delivery of goods, as measured by the current account, and assets, reflecting current account imbalances of earlier periods, to other countries. The net delivery of assets is to be understood in a broad sense, including real capital, shares, deposits, debentures, credit redemptions and other wealth titles. Accordingly, in Eurostat's balance of payments the Target and cash balances are counted as part of a country's net foreign investment position, and their increase is recorded as a public capital export treated in a way similar to fiscal and private capital exports.

The pooling of the NCBs' seignorage incomes in the Eurosystem implies that these balances bear an effective rate of interest, given that the intra-Eurosystem seignorage flows are direct implications of the Target and cash balances, which measure changes in the volumes of the NCBs' interest bearing sources and sinks of liquidity. More specifically, the effective rate of interest on Target and cash balances is a weighted average of the ECB's policy rates, where the weights are given by the structure of sources and sinks of the international liquidity flows measured by the Target and cash balances. There is even compound interest, as the intra-Eurosystem interest flow induced by pooling the seignorage incomes involves secondary international liquidity flows from the economies of the Target and cash balances debtors to the economies of the respective creditors, reshuffling central bank money between commercial banks' sources and sinks of liquidity as reported in the balance sheets of the NCBs. This secondary liquidity flow between the economies is itself booked in the Target balances, and it equilibrates the changes in these balance sheets. Thus, an initial change in the Target and cash balances will grow at the effective rate of interest, until it is serviced with countervailing transfers of goods and assets between the non-central bank sectors.

If a country with Target and cash balance liabilities leaves the Eurozone without respecting its obligations, the remaining countries suffer a real loss in terms of the present value of consumable wealth equal to the size of the leaving country's liabilities. In addition, the remaining countries may suffer from losing the purchasing power of bank notes in circulation as the leaving country is unlikely to be able to collect and return them.

Moreover, the Target and cash balance liabilities may be at risk if the banks and the governments, whose titles the debtor NCBs hold, default, because then this NCB may not be able to fulfill its statutory obligation to deliver to other NCBs the extra seignorage that would normally result from positive Target and cash balances. Thus, even though risk sharing is not foreseen by the statutes of the ECB and needs specific decisions by the ECB Council with each monetary program, the existence of negative Target and cash balances implies that the rest of the Eurosystem nevertheless does bear a credit risk measured by the size of these balances.

The Target and cash balance risk may not materialize directly because parliaments will set up rescue programs in time as well as international redistribution schemes to prevent insolvencies. As explained, this happened in the euro crisis since 2010 and during the Corona crisis of 2020. However, given that parliaments are no longer free after the prior decisions of the ECB's Governing

Council, the rescue payments may themselves be seen as an indirect materialization of the Target and cash balance risks.

The Target balances fluctuated substantially during the euro crisis because their volatility largely reflects net payment orders from capital flows, given the comparative sluggishness of goods flows.

Four phases of the euro crisis can be distinguished: The first phase was characterized by a sudden stop of private capital imports to, and subsequent capital flight from, the GIPSIC countries. During this phase the GIPSIC countries "printed" the money they could no longer borrow abroad. Local money printing and lending to domestic banks replaced the private capital that used to come in to finance current account deficits and it enabled the debtor countries to redeem their foreign debt. It also allowed foreign and domestic investors to sell their assets to local banks and other institutions that had benefitted from the NCBs' extra lending and send the proceeds abroad. The mechanism by which this asymmetry in the NCBs' money creation credits came about included using the scope left by the ANFA agreement as well as the scope opened up by national bank regulators in defining the assets eligible for the ECB's system of acceptable collateral and ELA credits. ELA credits are emergency credits that an NCB can provide at its own discretion, unless two thirds of the ECB's Governing Council object.

Eventually, the asymmetry in money creation and NCB lending had become so extreme in this first phase that the monetary bases of both Germany and Finland eventually consisted entirely of external money that had come in via payments from abroad.

The extreme asymmetry in money creation caused and necessitated by capital flows was sufficiently alarming to trigger the OMT promise of Mario Draghi's "whatever it takes", which constituted the second phase of the crisis. As the OMT basically was a free-of-charge credit default insurance, private capital risked returning to the crisis stricken countries. This involved payment orders that their NCBs had to fulfill, thus redeeming some of the intra-Eurosystem overdraft credit they had received before. The Target balances shrunk accordingly.

The third phase was characterized by the ECB's QE program that channeled €2.6 billion of extra liquidity into the markets, increasing the Eurozone's monetary base from €1.2 billion to €3.2 billion within only four years (after subtracting the banks' voluntary repayments of refinancing loans). Although the program was largely symmetrical and every NCB repurchased its own governments' bonds in proportion to country size (paid-in capital shares), the extra liquidity concentrated in just a few countries, primarily in Germany. The Target balances originating from this period can largely be seen as resulting from an extensive asset swap program, converting securitized and marketable domestic government debt into mere Target debt by the local NCB, which the creditors can never call due and carries only a small rate of interest, if any.

Arguably the deeper reason for the emergence of Target balances in both, period one and three, is that the ECB was unwilling to accept the risk spreads in interest rates required by markets, which reflected the differences in expected repayment probabilities. By setting equal policy interest rates for all countries of the Eurozone, it undercut the conditions that markets required for the countries of the Eurozone that they did not trust. Thus, with its policy of not differentiating the policy interest rates, the ECB induced private wealth owners to invest their money outside these countries, and banks to borrow from their respective NCBs rather than in the European interbank market. This all implied net payment orders to other countries and increased the Target balances.

This explains why the tiering decision of the ECB in September 2019 induced a halt and turnaround in the development of Target balances in the months following this decision. This was the fourth phase of the crisis. In essence, the ECB introduced an interest-free bracket or tier for the deposits that banks hold with their respective local NCB, six-fold the minimum reserve. As the penalty interest of currently -0.5% did not apply to deposits within the tier, the banks of northern countries, which had excess liquidity because of the inflow of liquidity as measured by the Target balances, lent some of it back to banks in the south, which typically had unused bracket space and hence faced a marginal deposit rate of zero. The effective differentiation of the marginal policy interest rates according to market preferences that resulted from tiering tended to reduce the imbalances in the Target and cash balances.

Phase four, in which the differentiation of policy interest rates dominated the Target balances was very short, however, as in March 2020 the Corona crisis eclipsed all other effects. All of a sudden, the euro crisis was back and an unprecedented capital flight to Germany took place that increased the German Target claim by €114 billion, while the Italian Target debt increased by €53 billion. The Corona crisis constitutes Phase five of the crisis. In many respects it resembles the first phase of the euro crisis, and the basic mechanisms described for that phase remain intact. However, given that it is likely to create the worst recession of the post-war period in the world economy, it may have implications that at this writing are difficult to predict. They range from the extremes of splitting the Eurozone to flooding the world economy with such enormous amounts of liquidity that subsequent inflation is likely plus, of course, anything in between.

13.2 The Pros and Cons of Target and Cash Balances

The question now is what these developments including the experience of the Eurozone since 2008 mean for the Target balances. Are these balances to be seen as useful ingredients of an optimally functioning currency union or are they deficiencies that urgently require a termination of Europe's currency union experiment? As we will see, neither is the case. There are instead good reasons for fixing the rules of the Eurosystem so as to correct the deficiencies.

The Pros

The advantage of Target balances is that they make the Eurosystem crisis-proof in the short run: The balances act as automatic shock absorbers and bail-out devices because, together with an elastic supply of local NCB credit, they shield the borrowers from shocks due to capital flight and the lenders from losing their claims. Countries in whose financial stability capital markets no longer trust are protected from becoming illiquid in international runs and fire sales because the public capital of the Eurosystem is always available as a replacement and escape helper of private capital. And what is more, given that foreign investors know that they always have an escape route once an economic situation becomes precarious, they dare to come in the first place. This ensures cheap credit for all members of the Eurozone including those with more unstable public and private finances.

To understand the merits of Target balances, suppose they are not allowed and abstract from current account reactions which would be sluggish anyway. In this case, a capital export by one group of investors would only be possible if there is other group of investors who are willing to import capital to the same amount or, alternatively, if there are private clearing houses (or international banks) that carry out the payment orders and accept open positions. An appropriate interest spread between the countries could ensure that the flight capital's willingness to escape is balanced by the clearing houses' willingness to finance the flight.

Unfortunately, however, in an economic crisis it is possible that there are no other investors or clearing houses that are willing to be the counterparts, whatever the interest spreads are. The reason is that higher nominal interest rates may induce local borrowers with limited equity capital to choose riskier projects with so much lower likelihood of success that the mathematical expectation of interest that can actually be paid does not increase but declines. This was convincingly demonstrated by Stiglitz and Weiss (1981) in general terms for any credit relationship between economic agents with asymmetric information.[1] In this case, there is an upper limit for the mathematical interest expectation that a crisis country is able to offer and hence there is no notional interest rate, agreed in a contract, at which a private clearing house would be willing to execute the counter transaction and carry out the necessary payment orders. The risk of credit rationing limits the usefulness of a private payments system based on clearing houses.

Such a system could be destabilizing in a crisis because foreign investors may rationally expect that the escape door will be closed if they exit too late. There could be fire sales of domestic assets, exacerbating the crisis and provoking a clearing house strike.

What is more, private investors foreseeing such risk may be reluctant to come in the first place or only at high rates of interest. Arguably that was the

---

[1] For the theory of excessive risk taking with limited liability and limited equity, see also Sinn (1980, 1983, 2009).

situation for some of the European countries before the euro was introduced. The reader may wish to revert to Fig. 10.1 in Chap. 10. High interest rates strangled the southern European countries, put a strain on public budgets and constrained investment and economic growth. As was argued there, this was the reason why these countries had desperately wanted to participate in the euro at the time, exerting maximal political pressure to be allowed in, even when they were unable to satisfy the debt/GDP entry condition of being below 60% required by the Maastricht Treaty.

The Cons

However, the Target balances also have significant downsides insofar as they inhibit the beneficial effect of interest spreads on borrowing behavior and the efficient allocation of capital across rivaling countries. Usually, creditors become nervous when a borrower cannot stop borrowing and keeps increasing his debt/income ratio. They fear that the borrower will not be able to repay and thus demand higher interest rates, which in turn curb the appetite for more debt. This is a natural debt brake which is essential not only for the functioning of private markets but also for federations such as the United States or Switzerland. In both countries, bail-outs of subordinated entities, states and cantons in particular, are legally excluded. The risk of bankruptcies is seen as a necessary ingredient of a functioning federalism, because it leads to more prudent borrowing behavior which, in fact, excludes such bankruptcies in the first place.

In Chap. 5 it was noted that the violation of this principle in the early decades of the United States had caused a bubble that burst in 1835, leaving in its wake 9 out of 29 states and territories bankrupt, augmenting the tensions because of the slavery problem and customs disputes that would eventually lead to the War of Secession. That experience laid the foundation for a system with strict budget constraints and fiscal discipline for the subunits of the American federation that has proved stable up to this day.

The Target balances are undermining the emergence of interest spreads by providing an incentive to NCBs to solve local financial problems with the printing press, exploiting the broad scope for idiosyncratic money printing that the statutes of the ECB and the decisions of the Governing Council leave. The NCBs may resort to extraordinary local money printing not only to boost their domestic economies via the stimulation of interest-dependent real investment, but also to provide private agents and the government with the liquidity necessary to buy foreign goods and assets and to redeem foreign debt. This was not only the case in the first phase of the crisis, as was shown in Fig. 5.1 and exemplified in the case of Greece. but also later, in Phase three, when symmetrical money creation under the QE program prevailed. It was possible in this phase to replace national government debt held in the portfolios of private foreign investors with Target debt in the Eurosystem by concentrating the new liquidity created in only a few countries, Germany in particular. Given that the Target system made such a private-public debt swap possible, it was rational for the crisis countries' NCB presidents sitting in the ECB's Governing Council to vote for an extensive QE program and potential repetitions.

These developments were problematic for at least two reasons. For one, the expectation of having access to the local printing press made cheap credit available and created an asset price bubble that would ultimately burst, as the Lehman crisis has shown, leaving overpriced torsos of once competitive economies in its wake. For another, Target balances, being quasi-fiscal credit, very similar to any credit that governments might provide each other on a bilateral basis or through rescue funds such as the ESM, lack a democratic justification. Genuine fiscal credits are being controlled and provided by parliaments after often painful considerations only. By contrast, the decisions leading to Target credits are made by a technocratic body, the ECB Governing Council, that is not authorized to carry out fiscal policy. This body has a biased democratic representation, given that the representatives of tiny countries like Malta, (southern) Cyprus and Luxembourg have the same voting power as the representatives of big countries like Italy, France or Germany.

Had this quasi-fiscal lending in the Eurosystem been foreseen by the parliaments when they decided on the euro in the Maastricht Treaty and subsequent treaties, the Target balances might perhaps even be acceptable from a legal perspective despite the fact that the decision making process of the Government Council is fundamentally undemocratic, with voting powers not having the remotest relationship to population size. However, the issue is mentioned nowhere in the treaties. Early articles by Garber (1998, 1999) referred to the transition phase up to the new currency rather than events after its introduction. Nowhere in the early documents can one find any hint that would suggest that Target would be more than an internal accounting system. As Schlesinger (2012) reports, imbalances in the Target system were simply not foreseen or discussed by central bankers, let alone by members of parliaments. They were never an issue.

Today they are an issue, however, given that the Target and cash balance credit in the Eurozone has risen way beyond a trillion euros (Fig. 1.2) and incurs a genuine investment risk similar to fiscal credits. The credit risk is real because the Target balances are not just irrelevant accounting items but result from the import of real goods and marketable assets. If no such goods and marketable assets are ever returned, the creditor countries suffer a loss in terms of the present value of consumption and living standard equal to the Target and cash balance claims.

The risk does not necessarily have to materialize in the form of a default or exit that devalues the Target and cash balances. To prevent such outcomes, the governments of the creditor countries may well decide to organize rescue programs, mutualization devices and transfer schemes that would channel fiscal credit, or publicly protected private credit, to the Target debtor countries and technically reduce the Target balances one to one. However, such measures may induce and enable capital flight from the debtor countries that mitigates or nullifies this effect on the Target balances, as was shown in Chap. 6 for the case of Greece.[2] In addition, these measures will eventually just shift the potential losses to other budgets without reducing their size. They help sustain the investors' portfolios and the living standard of the recipient countries, but continue to make these countries susceptible to the Dutch disease, because wages are kept at a level above the one compatible with international competitiveness. This would permanently undermine the competitiveness of their manufacturing sectors.

As the pros and cons are of similar economic importance, it neither follows that Target and cash balances should be forbidden nor that they should be allowed to grow without limits. Economic reason in the case of rivaling policy goals instead suggests that some interior solution between the extremes is to be sought, weighing the trade-offs between the rivaling goals of making the Eurosystem crisis-proof in the short run and in the long-run. The remainder of this book outlines the options for reasonable reforms of the Target system that might allow the Eurosystem to reach such an interior solution.

13.3 Reform Options

As the tiering decision of the ECB has shown, interest spreads are the key to avoiding Target balances. If the policy interest rates in the Target debtor countries increase beyond those in the creditor countries, banks in the latter loan out funds to banks in the former. This in itself reduces the Target balances and keeps their overall level in check. And if the spreads in market rates follow the increasing spreads in policy rates, it can be assumed that other private financial investors in Target creditor countries also lend more to institutions in the Target debtor countries. Thus rising interest spreads are the key for reducing the balances and the quasi-fiscal credit implications they have, including the bankruptcy risks for other members of the Eurozone.

Before a reform program can be implemented, it might be useful tough to accept the obvious and help over-indebted countries by debt moratoriums, given that were lured into their debt quagmires through the erroneous idea of equating nominal interest rates in the Eurozone. The debt moratoriums would have to provide relief for government debt, Target debt, cash balance debt and bank debt, so as to allow the afflicted countries to recover. Possibly these

---

[2] This is the reason why it would not be a solution to the Target problem if the NCBs of the Target creditor countries were allowed to buy assets such as gold (or securities of non-euro countries) abroad. Given that the Target balances result from a concentration of excess liquidity on countries that are considered safe, the extra liquidity injected into the Eurosystem by the gold purchases would come back to the Target creditor countries in exchange for real assets of these countries. Eventually, the creditor countries would just have swapped their own assets for gold, while their NCBs would have exchanged the gold for central bank money, with the Target balances remaining unchanged. A similar comment is appropriate for other schemes that have been designed to reduce the Target balances through politically organized purchases of foreign assets.

countries would also have to be given the chance of temporarily exiting the euro and returning later at a devalued currency ("breathing currency union").[3]

To bring about the necessary spreads in policy rates that would reduce the Target and cash balances, the first thing is that the ECB would have to accept that notional interest spreads are natural ingredients of a functioning capital market, because they are necessary to equate the true mathematical interest expectations, thus fulfilling the Law of one Price. The Law of one Price is the most fundamental law of economics, both in terms of a positive, if idealized, description of markets and in terms of allocative efficiency in the Pareto sense.

The question is how an incentive structure can be devised for the ECB to make this happen. This incentive structure involves two command lines or principal-agent problems, one from the ECB's Governing Council to the NCBs, and another one from elected parliaments to the Governing Council, re-defining the ECB's mandate and decision rules in a new EU treaty.

The first principal-agent problem can be solved in two possible ways. Theoretically, one is to resort to a system of ultra-tight monetary policy and allow local central banks to only symmetrically issue central bank money in their respective jurisdictions. This would mean that ELA and ANFA credit is no longer possible and that the full-allotment policy for refinancing loans that NCBs give to commercial banks is replaced with a policy of fixed allotments proportional to country size (paid-in capital key). To avoid credit rationing by NCBs, the ECB Council would have to tolerate policy interest rates to be differentiated sufficiently until the demand for central bank credit by banks equals the credit allotted to the respective NCBs. Target and cash balances would not be constrained in this case, however they would stay small, as for a country building up negative balances, the increasing liquidity shortage would automatically result in higher market rates, which makes it attractive for private foreign capital to come and mitigate this shortage. However, while feasible, such as system would be rigid and might also suffer from the Stiglitz-Weiss problem that, beyond some point, higher notional interest rates in a particular country would not necessarily attract more capital, as investors might not believe that they involve higher mathematical interest expectations due to excessively rising bankruptcy risks.

Thus, an arguably better possibility might be to impose brackets on the negative sum of Target and cash balances with penalty interest having to be paid by the debtor NCBs for amounts going beyond these brackets. Such a solution was recommended by Schlesinger (2012). The brackets would not imply a limit on transactions within the Eurozone, let alone capital controls or the like. They would, however, provide an incentive for the NCBs to keep the negative balances low, keeping local money supply tight and setting higher local policy interest rates. The penalty interest rates for excessive Target and cash balance liabilities would have to be sufficiently high to provide the necessary incentive.

---

[3] For an extensive discussion of the idea of a breathing currency union, see Sinn (2014a), pp. 337f.).

It could even be envisaged to have a staggered system of brackets with progressively increasing penalty interest rates on the Target and cash balance debt to allow for a smoother stabilization. Such a system of brackets with increasing penalty interest would resemble modern dynamic shock absorbers in cars that allow for comfortable gliding on normal roads and prevent the wheels from punching through the car's chassis on bumpy ones. Cars that have only springs and no shock absorbers are dangerously unstable on the road.

A hard rationing would not occur with this solution. For one, payment orders would never be restricted, and for another, at the expense of higher penalty interest on the excessive balances, more local refinancing credit could always be made available by the local NCB to replenish the liquidity losses due to international payment orders, if needed. However, as the public credit of the Eurozone would become progressively more expensive, less would be demanded and fewer net-payment orders to other countries would emerge.

The solution would work smoothly if the ECB Council could be expected to introduce and sustain a sufficiently rigid system of staggered brackets. That expectation may, however, be a bit too naive for a water-tight solution,

- given that the governing structure of the ECB Council is far from being a democratic representation and has a clear majority of countries with a negative net foreign asset position,
- given that its policies often turned out to be fiscal rescue operations rather than monetary in the conventional sense of the term[4] and
- given that the German Constitutional Court[5] voiced the suspicion that the ECB might have overstretched its mandate and does have the power to constrain the Bundesbank's to follow ECB commands.

Thus, a new EU treaty would be advisable in which the decision rules and the mandate of the ECB Council are changed to solve the second principal-agent problem. The essential ingredients of the new mandate to be defined for the ECB Council may require the following reforms.

1. The votes in the ECB Council represent paid-in capital keys for all decisions.
2. Decisions that involve a potential deviation from proportional money creation will have to be made with simple majority (rather than with only one third of the votes in the case of ELA credit today).
3. In addition to price stability and supporting the economic policy in general, provided it does not compromise the price stability goal, the ECB Council will be given the mandate of avoiding substantial balance-of-payments imbalances in the sense of Target and cash imbalances.

---

[4] Sinn (2014a, 2015a).
[5] Bundesverfassungsgericht (2014, 2017).

4. Excessive Target and cash balances in addition to some narrow margin to be fixed in the Treaty will have to be annually settled between the NCBs.

The most obvious means for settling the imbalances is gold. Gold has always been *the* universal means of transactions between central banks. In order to settle the balances with gold, it would not be necessary to have it on stock, no more than an investor who wants to reshuffle his portfolio needs to have money on stock. In order to settle the Target and cash balance debt, it is sufficient for an NCB or the state that owns it to sell other assets against gold and then use the gold to settle the debt. While unlimited Target and cash balances would remain possible and retain their functions as short-term overdraft credit aimed at providing liquidity help, gold settlement would ensure that the temporary overdraft credit could no longer be tacitly converted into a long-term fiscal loan without ever involving parliamentary decisions, as has been the case in the Eurozone.

Up to 1975, the twelve district Feds of the Federal Reserve System of the US had used gold to annually redeem the imbalances in their Interdistrict Settlement Accounts. Afterwards, they also allowed settlement with marketable assets that the Federal Reserve System had acquired in the open market operations.

In Europe, settlement with any kind of marketable assets would not be appropriate given that the Eurosystem is much younger than the Federal Reserve System and has not yet achieved a comparable stability of its subordinated member units. Moreover, of course, the Eurozone is far from being a nation state, which could be more indifferent to internal redistribution. Thus, the occasionally made proposal of handing over the assets bought with the QE program, mostly government bonds, to the Target and cash balance creditors is no viable solution. Such assets were typically overvalued, being bought way above the market price that would have prevailed without the purchases.

Things could be different if the EU developed further to an ordinary democratic state with a central, authoritative government having full control over the armed forces, foreign policy and intra-EU activities with externalities stretching across the old national borders. In that case a monetary system resembling that of the US, settling the imbalances with assets bought in the open market, might be suitable.

The proposed reforms would reinstall the hard budget constraints that any functioning economic system needs without throwing the baby out with the bathwater and destroying the benefits of a common European currency. The reforms would give the euro a reasonable chance to survive and, unlike the current system, would be compatible with a stable and prosperous economic development of the countries of Europe with the ultimate goal of creating a common state.

Acknowledgments The author gratefully acknowledges useful comments by Georg Milbradt and the publisher's anonymous referees as well as technical assistance by Anja Hülsewig, Christoph Zeiner, Paul Kremmel and Daniel Weishaar. The latter also added a number of useful comments.

Correction to: The Economics of Target Balances

CORRECTION TO:

H.-W. Sinn, *The Economics of Target Balances*,
https://doi.org/10.1007/978-3-030-50170-9

The original version of the chapters 5 and 12 was revised. In Chapter 12, on Page 103 of the book, the official German government data was corrected. In Chapter 5, On p. 36. the term "foreign exchange, equity" was replaced with "revaluation adjustments". The term STEPS market was changed to STEP market twice in the book, on p. 34 of Chapter 5, and on p. 145, right column. The chapter and book have been updated with the change.

The updated versions of the chapters can be found at
https://doi.org/10.1007/978-3-030-50170-9_5
https://doi.org/10.1007/978-3-030-50170-9_12

© The Author(s) 2021
H.-W. Sinn, *The Economics of Target Balances*,
https://doi.org/10.1007/978-3-030-50170-9_14

REFERENCES

Abelshauser, W. (2017), "Mythos Marshallplan", *ifo Schnelldienst* 70, no. 4, pp. 14–17.

AFP (2020), "Here is what Italy's New Financial Decree Means for Businesses", News Item, *The Local/AFP*, 7 April, https://www.thelocal.it/20200407/heres-what-Italys-new-financial-decree-means-for-businesses

Aizenman, J., Y.-W. Cheung and X. Qian (2019), "The Currency Composition of International Reserves, Demand for International Reserves, and Global Safe Assets", *NBER Working Paper* No. 25934, June.

Assenmacher, K., and S. Krogstrup (2018), "Monetary Policy with Negative Interest Rates: Decoupling Cash from Electronic Money", *IMF Working Paper* 191, August, https://www.imf.org/en/Publications/WP/Issues/2018/08/27/Monetary-Policy-with-Negative-Interest-Rates-Decoupling-Cash-from-Electronic-Money-46076

Bagehot, W. (1873), *Lombard Street. A Description of the Money Market*, Henry S. King & Co, London.

Banca d'Italia (2018), *Annual Report 2017*, 29 May, https://www.bancaditalia.it/pubblicazioni/relazione-annuale/2017/en_rel_2017.pdf?language_id=1

——— (2019), *Annual Accounts* 2018, 29 March, https://www.bancaditalia.it/pubblicazioni/bilancio-esercizio/2019-bilancio-esercizio/en-bil-eserc-2019.pdf?language_id=1

Berger, H., and A. Ritschl (1995), "Die Rekonstruktion der Arbeitsteilung in Europa. Eine neue Sicht des Marshall-Plans in Deutschland 1947–1951", *Vierteljahreshefte für Zeitgeschichte* 43, pp. 473–519.

Berchtold, E.-M., and Y. Sun (2019), *Chinesische Unternehmenskäufe in Europa. Eine Analyse von M&A-Deals 2006–2018*, Ernst & Young, https://www.ey.com/Publication/vwLUAssets/EY-Analyse_Chinesische_Investoren_in_Europa_2018/$FILE/EY-Analyse%20Chinesische%20Investoren%20in%20Europa%202018.pdf

Bini Smaghi, L. B. (2013), *Austerity: European Democracies against the Wall*, Centre for European Policy Studies, Brussels.

Borghi, C. (2019), " Salvini-Berater Borghi: ‚Der Euro ist die falsche Währung für Italien'" (interview), *Capital*, September, https://www.capital.de/wirtschaft-politik/salvini-berater-borghi-der-euro-ist-die-falsche-waehrung-fuer-italien

Brendel, M., and S. Jost (2013), "EZB leistet sich gefährliche Regelverstöße", *Welt Online*, 11 July, https://www.welt.de/wirtschaft/article115063852/EZB-leistet-sich-gefaehrliche-Regelverstoesse.html

Brendel, M., J. K. Eberl and C. Weber (2015), "Riskante Risikokontrolle", *ifo Schnelldienst* 68, no. 14, pp. 41–49, https://www.ifo.de/DocDL/sd-2015-14-weber-etal-risikokontrolle-2015-07-30.pdf

Buchheim, C. (1986), "Das Londoner Schuldenabkommen", in. L. Herbst, ed., *Westdeutschland 1945–1955. Unterwerfung, Kontrolle, Integration*, Oldenbourg, Munich, pp. 219–29.

Bundesministerium für Wirtschaft und Energie (2018), *Pressemitteilung—Außenwirtschaftsrecht*, 19 December, https://www.bmwi.de/Redaktion/DE/Pressemitteilungen/2018/20181219-staerkung-unserer-nationalen-sicherheit-durch-verbesserte-investitionspruefung.html

Bundesverfassungsgericht (2014), *Order of the Second Senate of 14 January 2014*, 2 BvR 2728/13, paras 1–24, https://www.bundesverfassungsgericht.de/SharedDocs/Entscheidungen/EN/2014/01/rs20140114_2bvr272813en.html;jsessionid=756FF5D90D864BEC48C059A50DF67C5F.1_cid394

——— (2016), *Headnotes to the Judgment of the Second Senate of 21 June 2016*, 2 BvE 13/13, paras. 99–102, 109, https://www.bundesverfassungsgericht.de/SharedDocs/Entscheidungen/EN/2016/06/rs20160621_2bvr272813en.html

——— (2017), *Order of the Second Senate of 18 July 2017*, 2 BvR 859/15, No. 1-137, https://www.bundesverfassun Princeton Essays in International Finance gsgericht.de/SharedDocs/Entscheidungen/EN/2017/07/rs20170718_2bvr085915en.html

Congressional Budget Office (2020), *CBO's Current Projections of Output, Employment, and Interest Rates and a Preliminary Look at Federal Deficits for 2020 and 2021*, Blog posted by P. Swagel, 24 April, https://www.cbo.gov/publication/56335

Corden, W.M., and J. P. Neary (1982), "Booming Sector and De-industrialisation in a Small Open Economy", *The Economic Journal* 92, pp. 825–48.

Chandler, L. V. (1958), *Benjamin Strong, Central Banker*, Brookings, Washington D.C.

Coeuré, B. (2017), *The International Dimension of the ECB's Asset Purchase Programme*, speech at the meeting of the Foreign Exchange Contact Group, 11 July, https://www.ecb.europa.eu/press/key/date/2017/html/ecb.sp170711.en.html

Conway, P. (1995), "Currency Proliferation: The Monetary Legacy of the Soviet Union", *Princeton Essays in International Finance* 197, June.

Cour-Thimann, Ph. (2013), "Target Balances and the Crisis in the Euro Area", *CESifo Forum* 14, Special Issue, https://www.ifo.de/DocDL/Forum-Sonderheft-Apr-2013.pdf

De Grauwe, P., and Y. Ji (2012), "What Germany Should Fear Most Is its Own Fear", *VoxEU*, 18 September, https://voxeu.org/article/how-Germany-can-avoid-wealth-losses-if-eurozone-breaks-limit-conversion-german-residents

Deutsche Bundesbank (2016), "Zur Bedeutung und Wirkung des Agreement on Net Financial Assets (ANFA) für die Implementierung der Geldpolitik", *Monatsbericht der Deutschen Bundesbank*, March, https://www.bundesbank.de/resource/blob/602250/cce2db20c5c583ddcd0fb4812e101ac3/mL/2016-03-agreement-on-net-financial-assets-data.pdf

——— (2019), *Geschäftsbericht 2018*, 27 February, https://www.bundesbank.de/resource/blob/779078/7948403e83979a08d7f49c93a59ed94e/mL/2018-geschaeftsbericht-data.pdf

Djankov, S. (2014), *Inside the Euro Crisis, An Eyewitness Account*, Columbia University Press, New York.

Doll, N., and T. Kaiser (2018), "Bund will Einfluss chinesischer Investoren gesetzlich begrenzen", *Welt online*, 7 August, https://www.welt.de/wirtschaft/article180694182/Firmenuebernahmen-Bund-will-Einfluss-chinesischer-Investoren-gesetzlich-begrenzen.html

Dorn, F., C. Fuest, M. Göttert, C. Krolage, S. Lautenbacher, S. Link, A. Peichl, M. Reif, S. Sauer, M. Stöckli, K. Wohlrabe and T. Wollmershäuser (2020), "Die volkswirtschaftlichen Kosten des Corona-Shutdown für Deutschland: Eine Szenarienrechnung", *ifo Schnelldienst* 73, no. 4, pp. 29–35.

Draghi, M. (2012), *Introductory Statement to the Press Conference* (with Q&A), 4 April, https://www.ecb.europa.eu/press/pressconf/2012/html/is120404.en.html

———. (2017), *Interrogazione con richiesta di risposta scritta QZ-120*, Letter to the Members of the European Parliament, Marco Valli and Marco Zanni, 18 January, https://www.ecb.europa.eu/pub/pdf/other/170120letter_valli_zanni_1.it.pdf?3ea18e5d94e7b94141581bc89c182772

Drechsler, I., Th. Drechsel, D. Marques-Ibanez and Ph. Schnabl (2016), "Who Borrows from the Lender of Last Resort?", *The Journal of Finance* 71, pp. 1933–74, https://doi.org/10.1111/jofi.12421

Eberl, J. K. (2016), *The Collateral Framework of the Eurosystem and its Fiscal Implications*, Dissertation, *ifo Beiträge zur Wirtschaftsforschung*, ifo Institut, Munich, https://www.ifo.de/DocDL/ifo-Beitraege_z_Wifo_69.pdf

Eberl, J. K. and C. Weber (2014), "ECB Collateral Criteria: A Narrative Database 2001–2013", *ifo Working Paper* No. 174, https://www.ifo.de/DocDL/IfoWorkingPaper-174.pdf

Eichengreen, B (2006), *Global Imbalances and the Lessons of Bretton Woods*, MIT Press, Cambridge.

Emminger, O. (1986), *D-Mark, Dollar, Währungskrisen. Erinnerungen eines ehemaligen Bundebankpräsidenten*, DVA, Stuttgart.

Eurogroup (2020), *Report on the Comprehensive Economic Policy Response to the COVID-19 Pandemic*, Press release, 9. April 2020, https://www.consilium.europa.eu/de/press/press-releases/2020/04/09/report-on-the-comprehensive-economic-policy-response-to-the-covid-19-pandemic/

European Central Bank (2001), *Decision of the European Central Bank of 6 December 2001 on the Allocation of Monetary Income of the National Central Banks of Participating Member States from the Financial Year 2002* (ECB/2001/16) (2001/914/EC), https://eur-lex.europa.eu/eli/dec/2001/914/2006-05-20

——— (2011), *Monthly Bulletin* 10, October, https://www.ecb.europa.eu/pub/pdf/mobu/mb201110en.pdf

——— (2012a), "Financial Reporting in the Eurosystem", *Monthly Bulletin* 4, April, pp. 87–98, https://www.ecb.europa.eu/pub/pdf/mobu/mb201204en.pdf

——— (2012b), *Guideline of the European Central Bank of 5 December 2012 on a Trans-European Automated Real-time Gross Settlement Express Transfer System (TARGET2)*, ECB/2012/27, 2013/47/EU, https://eur-lex.europa.eu/legal-content/EN/TXT/?uri=CELEX:32012O0027

——— (2014a), *Decision of the European Central Bank of 5 June 2014 on the Remuneration of Deposits, Balances and Holdings of Excess reserves* (ECB/2014/23) (2014/337/EU), Official Journal of the European Union, L 168, pp. 115–116, https://eur-lex.europa.eu/legal-content/EN/TXT/PDF/?uri=CELEX:32014D0023(01)&from=EN

—— (2014b), *Schriftliche Erklärung gemäß Art. 23 der Satzung des Gerichtshofs und Art. 96 der Verfahrensordnung des Gerichtshofs ...in der Rechtssache C-62/64*, 16 June 2014, unpublished document.

—— (2016a), *ECB Explains the Agreement on Net Financial Assets (ANFA)*, Press release, 5 February, https://www.ecb.europa.eu/press/pr/date/2016/html/pr160205.en.html

—— (2016b), *Agreement of 14 November 2014 on Net Financial Assets*, February, www.ecb.europa.eu/ecb/legal/pdf/en_anfa_agreement_19nov2014_f_sign.pdf

—— (2016c), *What is ANFA?*, ECB Homepage, 7 April, https://www.ecb.europa.eu/explainers/tell-me-more/html/anfa_qa.en.html

—— (2016d), *Convergence Report*, June, https://www.ecb.europa.eu/pub/pdf/conrep/cr201606.en.pdf

—— (2016e), *Economic Bulletin 7/2016*, p. 21, https://www.ecb.europa.eu/pub/pdf/ecbu/eb201607.en.pdf

—— (2016f), *European Union Balance of payments and International Investment Position, Statistical Sources and Methods*, "B.o.p. and i.i.p. book", November, https://www.ecb.europa.eu/pub/pdf/other/eubopintiinvposstmeth201611.en.pdf

—— (2016g), *Decision (EU) 2016/2248 of the European Central Bank of 3 November 2016 on the Allocation of Monetary Income of the National Central Banks of Member States whose Currency is the Euro* (ECB/2016/36), https://www.ecb.europa.eu/ecb/legal/pdf/celex_32016d003601_en_txt.pdf

—— (2019a), *Press Release*, 15 January, https://www.bde.es/f/webbde/GAP/Secciones/SalaPrensa/ComunicadosBCE/NotasInformativasBCE/19/fs190111en.pdf

—— (2019b), *Annual Report 2018*, 9 April, https://www.ecb.europa.eu/pub/pdf/annrep/ar2018~d08cb4c623.en.pdf

—— (2019c), *Account of the Monetary Policy Meeting of the Governing Council of the European Central Bank held in Frankfurt am Main on Wednesday and Thursday, 11–12 September*, https://www.ecb.europa.eu/press/accounts/2019/html/ecb.mg191010~d8086505d0.en.html

—— (2020a), *ECB Announces €750 billion Pandemic Emergency Purchase Programme (PEPP)*, Press release, 18 March, https://www.ecb.europa.eu/press/pr/date/2020/html/ecb.pr200318_1~3949d6f266.en.html

—— (2020b), *ECB Announces Package of Temporary Collateral Easing Measures*, Press release, 7 April, https://www.ecb.europa.eu/press/pr/date/2020/html/ecb.pr200407~2472a8ccda.en.html

—— (2020c), *Asset Purchase Programmes*, 16 April 2020, https://www.ecb.europa.eu/mopo/implement/omt/html/index.en.html

—— (2020d), *ECB Takes Steps to Mitigate Impact of Possible Rating Downgrades on Collateral Availability*, Press release, 22 April, https://www.ecb.europa.eu/press/pr/date/2020/html/ecb.pr200422_1~95e0f62a2b.en.html

European Court of Justice (2015), *Judgment of the Court (Grand Chamber) of 16 June 2015 Case C-62/14*, http://curia.europa.eu/juris/celex.jsf?celex=62014CJ0062&lang1=en&type=TXT&ancre=

—— (2018), *The ECB's PSPP Programme for the Purchase of Government bonds on Secondary Markets does not Infringe EU Law*, Press release No 192/18, based on

Judgment of the Court (Grand Chamber) of 11 December 2018, Case C-493/17, ECLI:EU:C:2018:1000, https://curia.europa.eu/jcms/upload/docs/application/pdf/2018-12/cp180192en.pdf

European Economic Advisory Group (2012), *The EEAG Annual Report of the European Economy: The Euro Crisis*, Eleventh Annual Report, CESifo, Munich, https://www.ifo.de/DocDL/EEAG-2012.pdf

——— (2013), *The EEAG Report of the European Economy: Rebalancing Europe*, CESifo, Munich, https://www.ifo.de/DocDL/EEAG-2013.pdf

European Parliament (2019), *Regulation (EU) 2019/452 of the European Parliament and of the Council of 19 March 2019 Establishing a Framework for the Screening of Foreign Direct Investments into the Union*, https://eur-lex.europa.eu/legal-content/EN/TXT/PDF/?uri=CELEX:32019R0452&from=EN

Eurostat (2010), *European Systems of Accounts (ESA 2010)*, https://ec.europa.eu/eurostat/documents/3859598/5925693/KS-02-13-269-EN.PDF/44cd9d01-bc64-40e5-bd40-d17df0c69334

faz.net (2012), "Reiche Griechen kaufen Wohnungen in Berlin", 17 December, http://www.faz.net/aktuell/wirtschaft/steigendeimmobilienpreise-reiche-griechen-kaufen-wohnungen-in-berlin-11996780.html

Federal Reserve Bank (2020), *Federal Reserve Takes Additional Actions to Provide up to $2.3 trillion in Loans to Support the Economy*, Press release, 9 April, https://www.federalreserve.gov/newsevents/pressreleases/monetary20200409a.htm

Focus Online (2011), "Reiche Griechen fliehen nach London", 4 November, http://www.focus.de/immobilien/kaufen/schuldenkrise-reiche-griechen-fliehen-nach-london_aid_681162.html

Fuest, C., and H.-W. Sinn (2015), "Die Risiken der Notkredite", *Ökonomenstimme*, 13 November, www.oekonomenstimme.org/artikel/2015/11/die-risiken-der-notkredite/

——— (2016), "Non tacemus", *Ökonomenstimme*, 18 January, www.oekonomenstimme.org/artikel/2016/01/non-tacemus/

——— (2018a), "Target-Risiken ohne Austritte", *ifo Schnelldienst* 71, no. 24, pp. 15–25, https://www.ifo.de/DocDL/sd-2018-24-fuest-sinn-target-risiken-2018-12-20.pdf

——— (2018b), "Target Risks without Euro Exits", *CESifo Forum* 19, no. 4, pp. 36–45, https://www.ifo.de/DocDL/CESifo-Forum-2018-4-fuest-sinn-target-december.pdf

——— (2019), "Die Regulierung der Banken macht die Target-Kredite nicht sicher", *SAFE Policy Blog*, 27 February, https://safe-frankfurt.de/de/policy-blog/details/die-regulierung-der-banken-macht-die-target-kredite-nicht-sicher.html

Garber, P. M. (1998), "Notes on the Role of Target in a Stage III Crisis", *NBER Working Paper* 6619, https://www.nber.org/papers/w6619.pdf

———. (1999), "The Target Mechanism: Will it Propagate or Stifle a Stage III Crisis?", *Carnegie—Rochester Conferences on Public Policy* 51, pp. 195–220, https://www.sciencedirect.com/science/article/pii/S0167223100000105

Gros, D. (2018), "How to Exit the Euro in a Nutshell—'Il Piano Savona'", *EconPol Europe Opinion* No. 8, June, Washington, D.C. http://www.econpol.eu/opinion_8

Hammermann, F., K. Leonard, P. Nardelli and J. von Landesberger (2019), "Taking Stock of the Eurosystem's Asset Purchase Programme after the End of Net Asset Purchases", *Economic Bulletin*, No. 2, 18 March, https://www.ecb.europa.eu/pub/economic-bulletin/articles/2019/html/ecb.ebart201902_01~3049319b8d.en.html

Hellwig (2015a), "Die EZB und die Deutschen in der Griechenlandkrise", *Ökonomenstimme*, 7 July, www.oekonomenstimme.org/artikel/2015/07/die-ezb-und-die-deutschen-in-der-griechenlandkrise

―――― (2015b), "Zur Diskussion um die Notkredite der griechischen Zentralbank für griechische Banken", *Ökonomenstimme*, 11 July, http://www.oekonomenstimme.org/artikel/2015/07/zur-diskussion-um-die-notkredite-der-griechischen-zentralbank-fuer-griechische-banken/

―――― (2015c), "Si tacuissent", *Ökonomenstimme*, 8 December, www.oekonomenstimme.org/artikel/2015/12/si-tacuissent/

―――― (2018a), "Wider die deutsche Target-Hysterie", *Frankfurter Allgemeine Sonntagszeitung*, no. 30, 29 July, pp. 20, https://www.faz.net/aktuell/finanzen/finanzmarkt/unberechtigte-panik-vor-italien-austritt-fuer-eurowaehrung-15712671.html

―――― (2018b), "Target-Falle oder Empörungsfalle?", *Perspektiven der Wirtschaftspolitik* 19, pp. 345–82, 10.1515/pwp-2019-0002

Hellwig, M. F., and I. Schnabel (2019), *Stellungnahme anlässlich der öffentlichen Anhörung des Finanzausschusses des Deutschen Bundestages zu den Anträgen der Fraktion der FDP und AfD zum Thema „Target"*, Bundestags-Drucksache 19/6416 and 19/9232), 5 June, https://www.bundestag.de/resource/blob/645586/3254e2723ad969f4cc8598adfa4d848c/08-Schnabel-data.pdf

Hoffmann, D. (2015), *Die EZB in der Krise. Eine Analyse der wesentlichen Sondermaßnahmen von 2007-2012*, Pro Business Verlag, Berlin.

――――. (2016a), "ANFA-Abkommen: Geheimhaltung nach 13 Jahren beendet", *BBL Betriebswirtschaftliche Blätter*, SparkassenZeitung, 8 July, https://www.sparkassenzeitung.de/medienmarkensuche/bbl-betriebswirtschaftliche-bl%C3%A4tter.html

――――. (2016b), "Erste Erkenntnisse zum ANFA-Abkommen: ANFA ermöglicht Finanzierung von Bankenabwicklungen durch nationale Zentralbanken", *ifo Schnelldienst* 69, no. 13, pp. 19–27, https://www.ifo.de/DocDL/sd-2016-13-hoffman-anfa-irland%20-2016-07-14.pdf

Homburg, S. (2011), "Anmerkungen zum Target2-Streit", in: H.-W. Sinn, ed., *Die europäische Zahlungsbilanzkrise, ifo Schnelldienst* 64, no. 16, Special issue, pp. 46–50, https://www.ifo.de/DocDL/ifosd_2011_16_9.pdf

――――. (2012), "Notes on the Target2 Dispute", in: H.-W. Sinn, ed., *The European Balance of payments Crisis, CESifo Forum* 13, Special issue, pp. 50–54, https://www.ifo.de/DocDL/forum-0112-special-9.pdf

――――. (2019a), "Speculative Eurozone Attacks and Departure Strategies", *CESifo Economic Studies* 65, no.1, pp. 1–15.

――――. (2019b), "Targetsalden sind nicht empörend, sondern gefährlich. Kommentar zum Beitrag von Martin Hellwig", *Perspektiven der Wirtschaftspolitik* 20, no. 2, pp, 98–102.

Ifo Institute (2012), *Bailing out Greece Means Haircuts Totalling 47 Billion Euros at the Expense of Public Creditors*, Press release, Munich, 7 December.

―――― (2014), *Further Relief Planned on Bailout Loans to Greece*, Press release, Munich, 11 February 2014.

Ilzetzki, E. (2014), "Comment on Whelan", *Economic Policy* 29, no. 77, pp. 125–30, http://www.hanswernersinn.de/dcs/Ilzetzki_Comment_on_Whelan_Target2-Balances_Economic_Policy_2014.pdf

International Monetary Fund (2009), *Balance of payments and International Investment Position Manual*, Sixth Edition (BPM6), IWF, Washington, D.C., https://www.imf.org/external/pubs/ft/bop/2007/pdf/bpm6.pdf
——— (2020a), *Policy Responses to COVID-19, Policy Tracker*, 10 April, https://www.imf.org/en/Topics/imf-and-covid19/Policy-Responses-to-COVID-19
——— (2020b), *World Economic Outlook*, April: Chapter 1, https://www.imf.org/en/Publications/WEO/Issues/2020/04/14/weo-april-2020
Istituto Nazionale di Statistica (2020), "Imprese e addetti", *Registro Statistico delle Imprese Attive (ASIA)*, http://dati.istat.it/
Italian Parliament (2019), *Parliament Motion 1/00013*, passed on 28 May 2019, https://aic.camera.it/aic/scheda.html?numero=1-00013&ramo=C&leg=18
James, H. (2010), "The Multiple Contexts of Bretton-Woods", *Oxford Review of Economic Policy* 28, 2010, pp. 411–30
———. (2012a), *Making the European Monetary Union*, Harvard University Press, Cambridge.
———. (2012b), "Alexander Hamilton's Eurozone Tour", *Project Syndicate*, 5 March,
———. (2012c), *Lessons for the Euro from History*, Speech at the conference European Crisis Historical Parallels and Economic Lessons, Julis-Rabinowitz Center for Public Policy and Finance, Princeton, 19 April, https://jrc.princeton.edu/sites/jrc/files/jrcppf_2012_-_james_-_paper.pdf
Kenen, P. B. (1991), "Transitional Arrangement for Trade and Payments among the CMEA Countries", *IMF Staff Papers* 38, June, pp. 235–67.
Keynes, J. M. (1943). "The International Clearing Union", speech delivered before the House of Lords, 18 May, reprinted in: S. E. Harris, ed., *Keynes' Influence on Theory and Public Policy*, A. A., New York 1950, pp. 359–68.
———. (1980), *The Collective Writings of John Maynard Keynes, XXV Activities 1940–1944: Shaping the Post-War World, The Clearing Union*, edited by D. Moggridge, Cambridge University Press, Royal Economic Society.
Krahnen, J. P, (2018), "Über Scheinriesen: Was TARGET-Salden tatsächlich bedeuten. Eine finanzökonomische Überprüfung", *Working Paper, White Paper Series, Research Center SAFE*—Sustainable Architecture for Finance in Europe, No. 56, Goethe University, Frankfurt, https://safe-frankfurt.de/fileadmin/user_upload/editor_common/Policy_Center/SAFE_White_Paper_56.pdf
———, (2019), "Target Balances and Financial Crises", *SAFE Policy Letter* No. 71, https://safe-frankfurt.de/fileadmin/user_upload/editor_common/Policy_Center/SAFE_Policy_Letter_71.pdf
Krugman, P. (2015), "The Austerity Delusion", *The New York Times*, 24 March, https://www.economics.utoronto.ca/gindart/2011-03-25%20-%20The%20austerity%20delusion.pdf
Lagarde, C. (2020a), *Introductory Statement to the Press Conference (with Q&A)*, 12 March 2020, https://www.ecb.europa.eu/press/pressconf/2020/html/ecb.is200312~f857a21b6c.en.html
———. (2020b), "ECB's Lagarde Walks Back Comments which Caused Italian Bond Yields to Spike" (interview), *CNBC*, 12 March, https://www.cnbc.com/2020/03/12/ecbs-lagarde-walks-back-comments-which-caused-italian-bond-yields-to-spike.html
Macron, E. (2017), *Initiative pour l'Europe—Discours d'Emmanuel Macron pour une Europe souveraine, unie, démocratique, Sorbonne Université*, Paris, 26 September,

https://www.elysee.fr/emmanuel-macron/2017/09/26/initiative-pour-l-europe-discours-d-emmanuel-macron-pour-une-europe-souveraine-unie-democratique

———. (2020), "Emmanuel Macron Says it is Time to Think the Unthinkable", *FT Interview*, Interviewers: V. Mallet and R. Khalaf, 16 April, https://www.ft.com/content/3ea8d790-7fd1-11ea-8fdb-7ec06edeef84

Michel, C. (2020), *Conclusions of the President of the European Council Following the Video Conference of the Members of the European Council*, 23 April 2020, https://www.consilium.europa.eu/en/press/press-releases/2020/04/23/conclusions-by-president-charles-michel-following-the-video-conference-with-members-of-the-european-council-on-23-april-2020/

Moggridge, D. (1980), ed, *The Collected Writings of John Maynard Keynes, XXV, Activities 1940.1944; Shaping the Post-War World, The Clearing Union*, Cambridge University Press, Cambridge UK.

Norges Bank (2019), *Government Pension Fund Global, Annual Report 2018*, 6 February, https://www.nbim.no/contentassets/02bfbbef416f4014b043e74b8405fa97/annual-report-2018-government-pension-fund-global.pdf

Potrafke, N., and M. Reischmann (2014), "Explosive Target Balances of the German Bundesbank", *Economic Modelling* 42, pp. 439–34.

Ratchford, B. U. (1941), *American State Debts*, Duke University Press, Durham.

Reinhart, C. (2017), "Overview Panel", 26 August, https://www.kansascityfed.org/~/media/files/publicat/sympos/2017/reinhart-remarks.pdf?la=en

———. (2018), "Italy's Long Hot Summer", Project Syndicate, 31 May, https://www.project-syndicate.org/commentary/Italy-sovereign-debt-restructuring-by-carmen-reinhart-2018-05?barrier=accesspaylog.

Reuters (2019), *Weidmann bekennt sich nun doch zum umstrittenen Euro Rettungsprogramm*, 19 June, https://de.reuters.com/article/bundesbank-weidmann-ezb-politik-idDEKCN1TK1LX

Rogoff, K. (2019), "Modern Monetary Nonsense", *Project Syndicate*, 4 March, https://www.project-syndicate.org/commentary/federal-reserve-modern-monetary-theory-dangers-by-kenneth-rogoff-2019-03?barrier=accesspaylog

Ruhkamp, S. (2012a), "Die Bundesbank fordert von der EZB bessere Sicherheiten", *faz.net*, 29 February, https://www.faz.net/aktuell/wirtschaft/schuldenkrise-die-bundesbankfordert-von-der-ezb-bessere-sicherheiten-11667413.html

———. (2012b). "Bundesbank geht im Targetstreit in die Offensive", *faz.net*, 12 March, https://www.faz.net/aktuell/wirtschaft/wirtschaftspolitik/f-a-z-gast beitragbundesbank-geht-im-targetstreit-in-die-offensive-11682060.html

Sachverständigenrat zur Begutachtung der Gesamtwirtschaftlichen Entwicklung (2018), *Vor wichtigen wirtschaftspolitischen Entscheidungen*, Annual Report18/19, https://www.sachverstaendigenrat-wirtschaft.de/fileadmin/dateiablage/gutachten/jg201819/JG2018-19_gesamt.pdf

Schlesinger, H. (2011), "Die Zahlungsbilanz sagt es uns", in: H.-W. Sinn, *Die europäische Zahlungsbilanzkrise, ifo Schnelldienst* 64, no. 16, Special issue, pp. 9–11, https://www.ifo.de/DocDL/SD-16-2011.pdf

———. (2012), "The Balance of payments Tells us the Truth", in: H.-W. Sinn, ed., The European Balance of Payments Crisis, *CESifo Forum* 13, Special issue, pp. 11–13, https://www.ifo.de/DocDL/forum-0112-special-2.pdf

Schöchli, H. (2012), "Standfest hinter der Nationalbank", *nzz.ch*, 18 July, http://www.nzz.ch/aktuell/wirtschaft/wirtschaftsnachrichten/standfest-hinter-der-nationalbank-1.17368206.

Scholze, A., and F. Westermann (2014), "Ein Kommentar zur Bilanzausweitung der Europäischen Zentralbank", *Universität Osnabrück, Working Paper* 102, December, https://www.wiwi.uni-osnabrueck.de/fileadmin/documents/public/2_institute/2.02_IEW/IEW_Working_Paper/WP_102.pdf

Schumacher, E. F. (1943). "Multilateral Clearing", *Economica* 10, pp. 150–65.

Seitz, F. (1995), "Der DM-Umlauf im Ausland", *Diskussionspapier* 1/95, Volkswirtschaftliche Forschungsgruppe der Deutschen Bundesbank, May, https://www.oth-aw.de/files/oth-aw/Professoren/Seitz/dkp199501.pdf

Sinn, H.-W. (1980), *Ökonomische Entscheidungen bei Ungewißheit*, Dissertation, J.C.B. Mohr (Paul Siebeck), Tübingen.

———. (1983), *Economic Decisions under Uncertainty*, North Holland, Amsterdam, New York and Oxford.

———. (2009), *Risk Taking, Limited Liability, and the Banking Crisis. Selected Reprints*, Ifo Institute, Munich.

———. (2011a), "Neue Abgründe", *Wirtschaftswoche* 8, 21 February, p. 35. English translation as an international press declaration of the Ifo Institute: "Deep Chasms", *Ifo Viewpoint* no. 122, 29 March 2011, http://www.hanswernersinn.de/archiv-hws/standpunkt/Ifo-Viewpoint-No%2D%2D122%2D%2DDeep-Chasms.html.1

———. (2011b), "Tickende Zeitbombe", *Süddeutsche Zeitung*, 3 April, https://www.sueddeutsche.de/geld/rettungsschirm-fuer-den-euro-tickende-zeitbombe-1.1080370

———. (2011c), "Die riskante Kreditersatzpolitik der EZB", *Frankfurter Allgemeine Zeitung* 103, 4 May, pp. 10, https://www.faz.net/aktuell/wirtschaft/konjunktur/target-kredite-die-riskante-kreditersatzpolitik-der-ezb-1637926.html

———. (2011d), "The ECB's Stealth Bailout", *VoxEU*, 1 June, https://voxeu.org/article/ecb-s-stealth-bailout

———. (2011e), "On and off Target" (reply to critics), *VoxEU*, 14 June, https://voxeu.org/article/and-target

———. (2012a), *Die Target-Falle—Gefahren für unser Geld und unsere Kinder*, Hanser, Munich.

———. (2012b), "Die Europäische Fiskalunion: Gedanken zur Entwicklung der Eurozone." (Sohmen Lecture), *Perspektiven der Wirtschaftspolitik* 13, pp. 137–78, http://www.hanswernersinn.de/dcs/2012_PWP13_Europaeische_Fiskalunion_Sohmen.pdf

———. (2012c), "Kurzvortrag zur Eurokrise vor dem Verfassungsgericht 10. Juli 2012", *ifo Schnelldienst* 65, no. 15, pp. 22–26, https://www.ifo.de/DocDL/ifosd_2012_15_2.pdf

———. (2012d), "Target Losses in Case of a Euro Breakup", *VoxEU*, 22 October, https://voxeu.org/article/target-losses-case-euro-breakup

———. (2013), *Verantwortung der Staaten und Notenbanken in der Eurokrise*, Expert opinion commissioned by the German Constitutional Court (Bundesverfassungsgericht), *ifo Schnelldienst* 66, Special issue, June, Revised Version November, https://www.ifo.de/DocDL/SD_Juni_2013_Sonderausgabe_1.pdf; abbreviated version also published in *Wirtschaftsdienst* 93, no. 7, 2013, pp. 451–54

———. (2014a), *The Euro Trap. On Bursting Bubbles, Budgets, and Beliefs*, Oxford University Press, Oxford.

———. (2014b), "Austerity, Growth and Inflation. Remarks on the Eurozone's Unresolved Competitiveness Problem", *The World Economy* 37, pp. 1–13; *CESifo Working Paper* No. 4086, January 2013.

———. (2015a), "Die EZB betreibt Konkursverschleppung", *Süddeutsche Zeitung*, 10 February, p. 18, http://www.hanswernersinn.de/dcs/ezb-konkursverschleppung-sz-10022018_0.pdf

———. (2015b), *Der Euro. Von der Friedensidee zum Zankapfel*, Hanser, Munich (revised Translation of Sinn 2014a).

———. (2015c), *Die griechische Tragödie*, ifo Schnelldienst 68, Special issue, 29 May, https://www.ifo.de/DocDL/SD_Mai_2015_SpecialIssue_1.pdf

———. (2015d), *The Greek Tragedy*, CESifo Forum 16, Special issue, June, https://www.ifo.de/DocDL/Forum-Special-2015-June_1.pdf

———. (2016a), *Der Schwarze Juni. Brexit, Flüchtlingswelle, Euro-Desaster—Wie die Neugründung Europas gelingt*, Herder, Freiburg, first and second edition 2016, third edition 2017.

———. (2016b), "Europe's Secret Bailout?", *Project Syndicate*, 28 November, www.hanswernersinn.de/en/PS_28112016

———. (2018a), "The ECB's Fiscal policy", *International Tax and Public Finance* 25, pp. 1404–33, https://link.springer.com/content/pdf/10.1007%2Fs10797-018-9501-8.pdf

———. (2018b), "Fast 1000 Milliarden Euro", *Frankfurter Allgemeine Zeitung* 163, 17 July, pp. 16, https://www.faz.net/aktuell/wirtschaft/konjunktur/das-target-saldo-der-bandesbank-liegt-bei-1000-milliarden-euro-15694675.html

———. (2018c), "Fast 1000 Milliarden Target-Forderungen der Bundesbank: Was steckt dahinter" (extensive version of Sinn 2018b), *ifo Schnelldienst* 71, no. 14, July, pp. 26–37, https://www.ifo.de/DocDL/sd-2018-14-sinn-target-2018-07-26.pdf

———. (2018d), *Target-Verluste bei Auflösung der Währungsunion und beim Kollaps eines nationalen Bankensystems* (Target losses if the currency union is dissolved or a national banking system collapses), Manuscript distributed to a macroeconomic discussion circle (Ökonomenrunde) sustained by C. C. von Weizsäcker (other authors anonymized according to Chatham house rules), 11 August, http://www.hanswernersinn.de/dcs/target-verluste-aufloesung-waehrungsunion-hws-11082018.pdf

———. (2019a), "The Effective Rate of Interest on Target Balances", *CESifo Working Paper* 7878, September, Munich, http://www.hanswernersinn.de/dcs/sinn-effective-rate-of-interest-target-cesifo-wp7878-2019_0.pdf

———. (2019b), "Der Streit um die Targetsalden.—Kommentar zu Martin Hellwigs Artikel 'Target-Falle oder Empörungsfalle?' ", *Perspektiven der Wirtschaftspolitik* 20, no. 3, pp. 170–214.

———. (2019c), "Warum die Targetsalden zurückgehen", *Frankfurter Allgemeine Zeitung*, 18. December, p. 17.

———. (2020), "Die Target-Salden schießen hoch. Die Kapitalflucht der Anleger aus den Mittelmeerländern erreicht in der Corona-Krise einen dramatischen Höchststand", *Süddeutsche Zeitung* 84, 9/10 April 2020.

Sinn, H.-W., and H. Feist (1997), "Eurowinners and Eurolosers: The Distribution of Seignorage Wealth in EMU", *European Journal of Political Economy* 13, pp. 665–89, http://www.hanswernersinn.de/dcs/sinn-ejpe-1997-eurowinners.pdf

Sinn, H.-W., and G. Sinn (1992), *Jumpstart. The Economic Unification of Germany*, MIT Press: Cambridge, MA, and London.

Sinn, H.-W., and F. Westermann (2001), „Two Mezzogiornos", *Rivista di diritto finanziario e scienza delle finanze* 60, pp. 29–54, http://www.hanswernersinn.de/en/publications/2001_RivistaFin60_Two_Mezzogiornos

Sinn, H.-W., and T. Wollmershäuser (2011), *Target-Kredite, Leistungsbilanzsalden und Kapitalverkehr: Der Rettungsschirm der EZB*, ifo Schnelldienst 64, Special issue, June, https://www.ifo.de/DocDL/ifosd-2011-Sonderausgabe1-20110624.pdf

——— (2012), "Target Loans, Current Account Balances and Capital Flows: The ECB's Rescue Facility", *International Tax and Public Finance* 19, pp. 468–508, https://link.springer.com/content/pdf/10.1007%2Fs10797-012-9236-x.pdf; updated version of *CESifo Working Paper* 3500, June 2011, and *NBER Working Paper* 17626, November 2011.

Snell, P. (2020), "What's Inside the Senate's $2 Trillion Corona-virus Aid Package", *NPR* (National Public Radio), 26 March, https://www.npr.org/2020/03/26/821457551/whats-inside-the-senate-s-2-trillion-coronavirus-aid-package?t=1586438555466

Skolimowski, P., and A. Speciale (2020), *ECB Buying Italian Bonds in Bid to Halt Market Rout*, Bloomberg, 18 March, https://www.bloomberg.com/news/articles/2020-03-18/ecb-is-said-to-buy-italian-bonds-in-bid-to-halt-market-rout

Spahn, P. (2019), "Targetsalden und die Vollendung der Währungsunion", *Perspektiven der Wirtschaftspolitik* 20, no. 2, pp. 103–06.

Steinkamp, S. (2019), "Wie dezentral sind Geldpolitik und Bankenaufsicht in Europa?", *Perspektiven der Wirtschaftspolitik* 20, no. 1, pp. 70–94.

Steinkamp, P., A. Tornell and F. Westermann (2017), "The Euro Area's Common Pool Problem Revisited: Has the Single Supervisory Mechanism Ameliorated Forbearance and Evergreening?", *CESifo Working Paper* 6670, September, https://www.econstor.eu/bitstream/10419/171134/1/cesifo1_wp6670.pdf

Steiner, A., S. Steinkamp, and F. Westermann (2019), "Exit Strategies, Capital Flight and Speculative Attacks: Europe's Version of the Trilemma", *European Journal of Political Economy* 59, pp. 83–96.

Stiglitz, J. E. (2014), "Europe's Austerity Zombies", *Project Syndicate*, https://www.universidadpermanente.com/iniciativas/sites/default/files/Europe_Austerity_Zombies_by_Joseph_E_Stiglit_Project_Syndicate.pdf

Stiglitz, J. E., and A. Weiss (1981), "Credit Rationing in Markets with Imperfect Information", *The American Economic Review* 71, no. 3, pp. 393–410.

Summers, L. H. (2019), "The Left's Embrace of Modern Monetary Theory is a Recipe for Disaster", *Washington Post*, 4 March. https://www.washingtonpost.com/gdpr-consent/?destination=%2fopinions%2fthe-lefts-embrace-of-modern-monetary-theory-is-a-recipe-for-disaster%2f2019%2f03%2f04%2f6ad88eec-3ea4-11e9-9361-301ffb5bd5e6_story.html%3f

Swiss National Bank (2019), "111th Annual Report 2018", 1 March, https://www.snb.ch/en/mmr/reference/annrep_2018_komplett/source/annrep_2018_komplett.en.pdf

Thiele, C.-L. (2013), *Deutsche Goldreserven*, Lecture given at press conference, 16 January, https://www.bundesbank.de/resource/blob/663410/b6ffe2f39e77f4e912916fe0e0093f11/mL/2013-01-16-pressegespraech-gold-thiele-praesentation-download.pdf

Tornell, A. (2018), *Eurozone Architecture and Target2: Risk-sharing and the Commonpool Problem*, UCLA, mimeo, https://static1.squarespace.com/static/5387a855e4b0422ca6699e71/t/5b8f5935cd8366875c3f5bdd/1536121142954/EurozoneTgt2+Tornell+March2018.pdf

Tornell, A., and F. Westermann (2011), "Greece: The Sudden Stop that Wasn't", *VoxEU*, 28 September, https://voxeu.org/article/Greece-sudden-stop-wasn-t

U.S. Department of Commerce, Bureau of the Census (1975), *Historical Statistics of the United States, Colonial Times to 1970*, part I, Bicentennial edition, Washington, D.C.
van Suntum, U. (2018), "The Truth on Target II", *CAWM Discussion Paper* 204, revised version, sent 21 August, https://www.wiwi.uni-muenster.de/cawm/sites/cawm/files/cawm/download/Diskussionspapiere/cawm_dp104.pdf
———. (2019), "Targetsalden und andere Risiken in der Europäischen Währungsunion", *Perspektiven der Wirtschaftspolitik* 20, no. 2, pp. 107–14.
Varoufakis, J. (2015), "Deescalating Europe's Politics of Resentment", *Project Syndicate*, 25 March, https://www.project-syndicate.org/commentary/greek-bailout-restructuring-by-yanis-varoufakis-2015-03?barrier=accesspaylog
Weber, Ch. (2016), *The Collateral Policy of Central Banks—An Analysis Focusing on the Eurosystem*, Ph.D. dissertation, *ifo Beiträge zur Wirtschaftsforschung*, Ifo Institute, Munich, https://www.ifo.de/DocDL/ifo_Beitraege_z_Wifo_72.pdf
Westermann, F. (2014a), "Comment on Whelan", *Economic Policy* 29, no. 77, January, pp. 117–25, www.hanswernersinn.de/dcs/Westermann_Comment_on_Whelan_Target2-Balances_Economic_Policy_2014_0.pdf
———. (2014b), "Discussion of TARGET2 and Central Bank Balance sheets", *Working Paper* 99, University of Osnabrück, Institute for Empirical Economic Research, February, www.wiwi.uni-osnabrueck.de/fileadmin/documents/public/2_institute/2.02_IEW/IEW_Working_Paper/WP_99.pdf
———. (2016a), "ECB Target-2 Balances Keep Rising. Governing Council Must Consider QE Risks", *OMFIF*, 29 November, http://www.eurocrisismonitor.com/
———. (2016b), "Die Nebenwirkungen der expansiven Geldpolitik nehmen zu", *Ökonomenstimme*, 7 December, http://www.oekonomenstimme.org/artikel/2016/12/die-nebenwirkungen-der-expansiven-geldpolitik-nehmen-zu/
Whelan, K. (2014), "TARGET2 and Central Bank Balance sheets", *Economic Policy* 29, no. 77, pp. 79–137, https://doi.org/10.1111/1468-0327.12025
Whittaker, J. (2011), "Eurosystem Debts, Greece, and the Role of Banknotes", *Lancaster University Working Paper*, 14 November, https://mpra.ub.uni-muenchen.de/38406/1/MPRA_paper_38406.pdf
Wolf, T., and J. Odling-Smee (1994), *Financial Relations among Countries of the Former Soviet Union*, IMF Economic Reviews 1, International Monetary Fund, Washington DC.
Wollmershäuser, T. (2020), "ifo Konjunkturprognose Frühjahr 2020: Konjunktur bricht ein", *ifo Schnelldienst Digital* 73, no. 1, pp. 1–9.
Wolman, A. L. (2013), "Federal Reserve Interdistrict Settlement", *Economic Quarterly* 99, pp. 117–41.
World Trade Organization (2020), *Trade Set to Plunge as COVID-19 Pandemic upends Global Economy*, Press release, Geneva, 8 April 2020, https://www.wto.org/english/news_e/pres20_e/pr855_e.pdf
Wright, R. E. (2008), "Cementing the Union", *Financial History*, Spring 2008, pp. 14–18.

Statistical References

Banca d'Italia, Annual Accounts, Balance Sheets, https://www.bancaditalia.it/pubblicazioni/bilancio-esercizio/index.html

Banco de España, Annual Accounts, Balance Sheets, https://www.bde.es/bde/en/secciones/informes/Publicaciones_an/cuentas-anuales-/

Bank of Greece, Financial Statements, https://www.bankofgreece.gr/en/news-and-media/financial-statements

Deutsche Bundesbank, Balance Sheets, https://www.bundesbank.de/en/statistics/macroeconomic-accounting-systems/balance-sheets

Deutsche Bundesbank, Banken und andere finanzielle Unternehmen, Banken, Bilanzpositionen, Bankstatistische Gesamtrechnungen, Bankstatistische Gesamtrechnungen in der Europäischen Währungsunion, Liquiditätsposition des Bankensystems, https://www.bundesbank.de/de/statistiken/zeitreihen-datenbanken

Deutsche Bundesbank, Geldpolitische Geschäfte des Eurosystems (Tenderverfahren), https://www.bundesbank.de/resource/blob/607812/56b28363cb29bd223e1cd202f62e4bfb/mL/refd-data.pdf

Deutsche Bundesbank, Statistiken, Zeitreihen-Datenbanken: Außenwirtschaft, Auslandsvermögen und -verschuldung (lt. Statistischer Fachreihe), Auslandsposition der Bundesbank, https://www.bundesbank.de/de/statistiken/zeitreihen-datenbanken

European Central Bank, Capital Subscription, https://www.ecb.europa.eu/ecb/orga/capital/html/index.en.html

European Central Bank, Eurosystem balance sheet, https://sdw.ecb.europa.eu/browse.do?node=9691110

European Central Bank, Eurosystem Consolidated Statement, http://sdw.ecb.europa.eu/browse.do?node=9691294-

European Central Bank, Minimum Reserves and Liquidity, https://sdw.ecb.europa.eu/browse.do?node=9691110

European Central Bank, Statistical Data Warehouse, ECB/Eurosystem Policy and Exchange Rates, https://sdw.ecb.europa.eu/browse.do?node=9691097

European Central Bank, Statistical Data Warehouse, Target Balances of Participating NCBs, https://sdw.ecb.europa.eu/browse.do?node=9691112

European Central Bank, Weekly Financial Statements, https://www.ecb.europa.eu/press/pr/wfs/2020/html/index.en.html

European Commission, EU Budget, https://ec.europa.eu/info/strategy/eu-budget_en

European Commission, The Economic Adjustment Programme for Greece: Fifth Review, https://ec.europa.eu/economy_finance/publications/occasional_paper/2011/op87_en.htm

European Financial Stability Facility, Lending Operations

European Stability Mechanism, Governance, Shareholders, https://www.esm.europa.eu/efsf-governance

Eurostat, Database, Economy and Finance, Balance of payments—International Transactions, https://ec.europa.eu/eurostat/data/database

Eurostat, Database, Economy and Finance, National Accounts (ESA 2010), Annual National Accounts, Annual Sector Accounts (ESA 2010), Non-financial Transactions, https://ec.europa.eu/eurostat/data/database

——— 2010), Annual National Accounts, Main GDP Aggregates, GDP and Main Components, https://ec.europa.eu/eurostat/data/database

Eurostat, Database, Industry, Trade and Services, Short-term Business Statistics, Industry, Production in Industry, https://ec.europa.eu/eurostat/data/database

European Union, Protocol (no 4) on the Statute of the European System of Central Banks and of the European Central Bank, https://www.ecb.europa.eu/ecb/legal/pdf/c_32620121026en_protocol_4.pdf

International Monetary Fund, Financial Activities, http://www.imf.org/cgi-shl/create_x.pl?fa+2012

International Monetary Fund, Financial Soundness Indicators (FSIs), GFSR FSI Tables, Bank Non-performing Loans to Total Loans, https://data.imf.org/?sk=51B096FA-2CD2-40C2-8D09-0699CC1764DA

International Monetary Fund, SDR Exchange Rate Archives by Month, https://www.imf.org/external/np/fin/data/param_rms_mth.aspx

National Bureau of Economic Research, NBER Macrohistory: XI. Securities Markets, Germany, Index of Stock Prices 01/1870-12/1913, https://data.nber.org/databases/macrohistory/contents/chapter11.html

Thomson Reuters Datastream, Interest Rates, Benchmark Bonds

Yahoo Finance, https://finance.yahoo.com/quote/%5EGSPC/history?period1=-1325462400&period2=1587081600&interval=1mo&filter=history&frequency=1mo

Index[1]

A
Abelshauser, W., 42
Agreement on Net Financial Assets (ANFA), 35, 36, 39, 41, 58, 63n7, 64, 67n12, 69, 70n16, 85, 111, 117, 123
Aizenman, J., 16
Americans, 94
Anstaltslast, 103
Asian Crisis, 95
Assenmacher, K., 57
Asset Purchase Programme (APP), 53, 57, 58, 91
Austerity, 46
Austria, 1, 93

B
Bagehot, W., 37
Balance of payments (b.o.p), 4, 16–19, 21, 27, 28, 40, 62, 66, 103, 116, 124
Balance sheet, 1–3, 25, 27, 28, 30, 34, 41, 56, 62, 64, 71–72, 78–80, 79n25, 102, 106–108, 116
Banca d'Italia, 3, 14, 30, 56–58, 95–97, 106
Banco de España, 2, 30, 35, 56, 59

Bancor, 21
Bank for International Settlements in Basel (BIS), 21
Bankruptcies, 5, 37, 91, 97, 108–112, 120
Banque de France, 15
Base money, 13, 33, 36, 49–52, 54, 56, 58, 72, 80, 109, 110
Belgium, 1, 105
Berchtold, E.-M., 59
Berger, H., 42
Berlusconi, Silvio, 5, 90, 104
Bini Smaghi, L. B., 5, 91, 104
Borghi, C., 104
Brendel, M., 34
Bretton Woods, 21–23
Buchheim, C., 42
Budget constraints, 20, 120, 125
Bulgaria, 2, 3, 9
Bundesbank, 2, 3, 12–16, 21–23, 25, 26, 29, 30, 32, 35, 36, 51, 52, 56, 59, 60, 62, 62n4, 63n5, 64n10, 70n16, 71–72, 96, 102, 103, 106, 124
Bundesministerium für Wirtschaft und Energie, 60
Bundesverfassungsgericht, 53, 103, 124

---

[1] Note: Page numbers followed by 'n' refer to notes.

C

Capital controls, 38, 39
Capital export, 4, 11, 17–20, 28, 46, 116, 119
Capital flight, 17–20, 31, 33, 36, 37, 41, 45–47, 54, 72, 76, 96, 97, 107, 117–119, 121
Capital import, 18–20, 22, 28, 117
Capital keys, 63, 108, 123
Cash balances, 18, 25–27, 50
Chandler, L. V., 85
China, 7, 93
Clearing house, 20, 119
Coeuré, B., 56, 59
Collateral, 13, 20, 34–37, 39, 41, 85, 98, 99, 117
Congressional Budget Office, 97
Consols, 14
Conway, P., 22
Corden, W.M., 113
Corona crisis, 2, 3, 7, 32, 93–99, 102, 104, 116, 118
Coronavirus, 92
The Council for Mutual Economic Assistance (COMECON), 22
Cour-Thimann, Ph., 10, 30
Credit constraint, 20
Credit rationing, 119, 123
Croatia, 2, 3, 9
Current account deficit, 17–19, 22, 28, 31, 33, 37, 40, 43–46, 55, 87, 117
Cyprus, 2, 20, 25, 30, 121
Czech Republic, 2, 9
Czechia, 3

D

De Grauwe, P., 75n21, 104
Demand deposits, 23, 32, 56, 63, 68, 70–72
Denmark, 2, 3, 9
Deposit facility rate, 68, 70–72, 76, 77, 81, 85, 86
d'Italia, 58
Djankov, S., 5, 91
Doll, N., 60
Dorn, F., 94
Dot-com Bubble, 95
Dow Jones Index, 94

Draghi, M., 4, 13, 32, 104, 105, 117
Drechsler, I., 34, 35
Dual currency, 57
Dutch disease, 112–113

E

Eberl, J. K., 34, 35
ECB Council, 1, 13, 70, 86, 87, 116, 123, 124
Effective marginal rate of interest, 87–88
Eichengreen, B., 21
ELA loans, 35
Emergency Liquidity Assistance (ELA), 36, 39, 41, 45, 63n7, 64, 69, 85, 111, 117, 123, 124
Emminger, O., 22
EU Commission, 41
Eurogroup, 98
European Central Bank (ECB), 1–3, 13, 26, 30, 32, 35, 40, 53, 54, 62n2, 62n3, 63, 63n5, 63n6, 64, 64n10, 69n14, 70n18, 71–72, 78n24, 79n25, 90, 91, 98, 99, 103
European Court of Justice, 53, 90
European Economic Advisory Group, 19, 37, 85
European Financial Stabilisation Mechanism (EFSM), 40
European Financial Stability Facility (EFSF), 31, 42
European Financial Stability Mechanism (EFSM), 42
European Investment Bank (EIB), 31, 54, 69n15, 98
European Monetary Agreement, 22
European Parliament, 60
European Payments Union (EPU), 21
European Stability Mechanism (ESM), 31, 32, 40, 42, 53, 54, 98, 121
Eurostat, 4, 6, 15, 18, 40, 47, 102, 116
Eurozone crisis, 4–7, 86
Eurozone deposit insurance (EDIS), 112
Excess liquidity, 32, 33, 50, 68, 70–73, 76, 77, 79, 85, 88, 91, 92, 118
Excess reserves, 70–72, 77, 85, 86
External money, 50

F
Faz.net, 45
Federal Funds Rate, 85
Federal Reserve Bank, 10, 12, 21, 30, 98
Federal Reserve Bank of New York, 10
Federal Reserve District of New York, 29
Federal Reserve System (Fed), 10, 13, 14, 125
Feist, H., 26
Financial crisis, 4, 5, 30, 36, 89, 93
Financial Times, 99
Finland, 2, 30, 51, 54, 105, 117
First principal-agent problem, 123
Fiscal capital flow, 18
Fiscal policy, 121
Flight of capital, 20
Focus Online, 45
Foreign investment position, 43
Founders' Crisis, 95
France, 1, 5, 15, 27, 31, 42, 43, 93, 98, 99, 105, 106, 121
French, 94
Fuest, C, 25, 63n8, 69, 70n16, 75, 108, 111

G
Garber, P. M., 37, 121
German Constitutional Court, 103
German Council of Economic Advisors, 79n26
Germans, 94
Germany, 1, 2, 5, 15, 16, 18, 19, 21, 23, 26–28, 30–32, 42, 43, 51–54, 56, 58–60, 80, 88, 91, 94–97, 103, 105–107, 113, 117, 118, 120, 121
Gold, 10, 11, 13, 21–23, 69, 78, 84, 122, 125
Gold reserves, 22
Gold settlement, 10, 21, 84, 125
Gold to settle the debt, 125
Governing Council, 13, 14, 33–36, 39, 88, 90–92, 106, 110, 111, 116–117, 120, 121, 123
Government bond, 5, 14, 15, 23, 30, 34, 41, 54–60, 69, 69n15, 87, 89, 95–99, 103, 108, 125
Government Council, 121

Great Depression, 94, 95
Great Recession, 94
Greece, 1, 5, 15, 16, 18, 20, 25, 28, 30, 34, 38–47, 90, 105, 106, 111, 120, 122
Greece, Ireland, Portugal, Spain, Italy and Cyprus (GIPSIC), 30, 35, 117
Gros, D., 104

H
Hamilton, Alexander, 37
Hammermann, F., K., 53
Harberger, 37
Hellwig, M. F., 15, 62n1, 63n8, 63n9, 70n16, 104
Hoffmann, D., 35
Homburg, S., 4, 19, 26, 50, 104, 106
Hungary, 2, 3, 9

I
Ifo Institute, 42, 62, 62n4
Ilzetzki, E., 16
Inflation, 5, 31, 57, 110
Insolvencies, 37, 111, 112, 116
Interbank market, 5, 11, 31, 78, 87, 90, 118
Interdistrict Settlement Account (ISA), 29, 125
Interdistrict Settlement System (ISA), 10, 21
Interest spreads, 5, 37, 84, 88, 90, 119, 120, 122, 123
Internal money, 50
International Bank for Economic Co-operation (IBEC), 22
International-investment-position (i.i.p.), 18
International Monetary Fund (IMF), 3, 27–28, 30, 40–42, 91, 94, 98
Intra-Eurosystem interest, 103
Ireland, 1, 6, 16, 27, 30, 31, 34
ISA balances, 84
Istituto Nazionale di Statistica, 5
Italian Mezzogiorno, 113
Italian Parliament, 104
Italians, 94

Italy, 1, 5, 7, 14–16, 28, 30–34, 54, 55, 57–59, 88, 90, 91, 93, 96, 98, 104–106, 113, 121

J
James, H., 21, 37
Ji, Y., 104

K
Kaiser, T., 60
Kenen, P. B., 22
Keynes, J. M., 21
Keynesian, 5, 37, 97
Krahnen, J. P, 107, 108
Krogstrup, S., 57
Krugman, P., 46

L
Lagarde, C., 92
Law of one Price, 90, 123
Lega, 105
Lehman Brothers, 95
Lehman crisis, 1, 5, 6, 13, 18, 19, 43, 94, 96, 97, 121
Longer Term Refinancing Operations (LTROs), 34, 54, 69
Luxembourg, 30, 31, 56, 75, 121

M
Maastricht Treaty, 5, 11, 12, 53, 60, 103, 120, 121
Macron, E., 99, 113
Madrid Summit 1995, 88
Main refinancing rate, 68
Malta, 75, 121
Marginal effective intra-Eurosystem rate of interest on Target and cash balances, 68
Marginal effective rate of interest, 73, 74
Marginal effective rate of interest on target and cash balances, 67–72
Marshall credits, 42
Marshall Fund, 42
Michel, C., 98

Minimum reserves, 32, 50, 64, 68, 70–73, 76, 77, 79, 85, 86, 118
Modern Monetary Theory (MMT), 104, 110
Moggridge, D., 21
Monetary assets, 68
Monetary bases, 49–52, 54, 68, 69, 73, 75, 117
Monetary policy transmission, 37
Money creation credit, 14, 33, 41, 45, 50, 58, 64–66, 68, 72, 73, 75–77, 79, 80, 84, 108, 117
Money-in-the-window theory, 37

N
Neary, J.P., 113
Net payment orders, 1, 2, 9, 17, 36, 41, 55, 56, 78, 84, 117, 118
Netherlands, 2, 30, 54, 56, 105, 107, 113
New Year's festival, 93
Norges Bank, 23
Norway, 13
Norwegian Sovereign Wealth Fund, 23

O
Odling-Smee, J., 22
Open market operations, 10, 13, 50, 51, 125
Outright Monetary Transactions (OMT), 32, 53, 54, 85, 89–91, 112, 117
Overdraft, 15, 19, 45
Overdraft credit, 10, 117, 125
Overdraft loans, 115

P
Paid-in capital share, 105
Paid-in equity capital, 50
Pandemic Emergency Purchase Programme (PEPP), 92, 96, 98
Papandreou, Geiorgios A., 5, 90
Pareto, 123
Payment orders, 33
Penalty interest, 32, 86, 88, 118, 123, 124

Poland, 2, 3, 9
Policy interest rates, 61, 63, 64, 68, 70–73, 77, 79, 84–88, 92, 118, 122, 123
Pooling, 2, 63–66, 69–70, 73–78, 80, 83, 102–104, 107, 109, 116
Portugal, 1, 5, 15, 16, 27, 30, 34, 46, 88
Potrafke, N., 31
Pre-Lehman, 112
Price stability, 14, 124
Primary interest, 64
Primary seignorage income, 64, 67–72
Principal-agent problems, 123
Private capital flow, 14, 18, 84, 85, 95–96
Public Sector Purchase Programme (PSPP), 53, 54, 63n7, 64, 70n16, 92, 111

Q

Quantitative Easing (QE), 26, 32, 33, 51, 53, 54, 56–60, 72, 81, 85–87, 91, 96, 97, 117, 120, 121, 125

R

Ratchford, B. U., 37
Redistribution gain, 67
Reinhart, C., 15
Reischmann, M., 31
Reuters, 89
Ritschl, A., 42
Rogoff, K., 110
Romania, 2, 3, 9
Ruhkamp, S., 13

S

Sachverständigenrat, 79n26
Salvini, 104
S&P 500, 95
Savona, 104
Schlesinger, H., 4, 12, 63n5, 121, 123
Schnabel, I., 63n9, 104
Schöchli, H., 23
Scholze, A., 62n2
Schumacher, E. F., 21
Secondary interest, 64
Secondary seignorage income, 64, 67–72
Second principal-agent problem, 124
Securities Markets Programme (SMP), 30, 41, 58, 85
Seignorage, 2, 64–68, 67n13, 74, 75, 78, 80, 83, 102, 103, 105, 107–111, 116
Seignorage income, 64
Seignorage wealth, 26, 103
Seitz, F., 26
Settle the balances with gold, 125
Settling the imbalances, 125
Sinn, H.-W., 3, 4, 6, 7, 10–12, 15, 16, 18, 19, 22, 25, 26, 30, 31, 33–37, 39, 40, 45, 50, 51, 55, 59, 62n4, 63n8, 63n9, 67n11, 69, 70n16, 71–72, 75, 75n21, 76n22, 79n26, 85, 86, 96, 102, 104, 106, 108, 111, 113, 119, 123, 124
Skolimowski, P., 97
Snell, P., 97
Spahn, P., 104
Spain, 1, 5, 7, 15, 16, 30–32, 34, 54, 88, 93, 96
Spaniards, 94
Speciale, A., 97
Statute of the European System of Central Banks and of the European Central Bank, 69n14
Statutory amount of bank notes in circulation, 107
Statutory amount of cash, 72
Statutory stock of money balances, 50
Steiner, A., 18, 19
Steinkamp, S., 34, 35
STEP market, 34
Stiglitz, J. E., 20, 46, 119
Stiglitz-Weiss, 123
Stock market, 3, 32, 92, 94, 95, 98
Stock market crashes, 95
Summers, L. H., 110
Summit, 98
Summit of Madrid, 5
Sun, Y., 59
Swap line arrangements, 16
Sweden, 2, 3, 9
Swiss central bank, 23
Swiss currency, 23
Swiss National Bank, 23
Switzerland, 13, 23, 120

T
Target, 1
Targeted Longer Term Refinancing Operations (TLTROs), 55
Term deposit rate, 68
Thiele, C.-L., 22
Tier, 71–72, 85, 118
Tiering, 83–92, 97, 118
Tiers, 32
Tornell, Aaron, 16
Transfer ruble, 22
Transmission of monetary policy, 92
Treaty on the Functioning of the European Union (TFEU), 11, 12, 37, 53, 55, 60, 103

U
United Kingdom, 21
United States (US), 4, 7, 10, 37, 120
US, 56, 84, 94, 125
U.S. Department of Commerce, 94

V
van Suntum, U., 63n8, 104
Varoufakis, Yanis, 38, 42–44, 46
von Weizsäcker, C. C., 108

W
Weber, C., 34, 35
Weidmann, Jens, 13, 60
Weiss, A., 20, 119
Westermann, F., 4, 16, 54, 59, 62n2, 91, 113
Whelan, K., 16
Whittaker, J., 25, 26
Wolf, T., 22
Wollmershäuser, T., 3, 4, 12, 15, 16, 18, 19, 30, 33, 36, 50, 76n22, 94
Wolman, A. L., 10, 30
World Trade Organization (WTO), 94
Wright, R. E., 37

Y
Yahoo Finance, 95

GPSR Compliance

The European Union's (EU) General Product Safety Regulation (GPSR) is a set of rules that requires consumer products to be safe and our obligations to ensure this.

If you have any concerns about our products, you can contact us on

ProductSafety@springernature.com

In case Publisher is established outside the EU, the EU authorized representative is:

Springer Nature Customer Service Center GmbH
Europaplatz 3
69115 Heidelberg, Germany

www.ingramcontent.com/pod-product-compliance
Lightning Source LLC
LaVergne TN
LVHW010342260326
834688LV00036B/844